My Nun

and Her Husband

Milam McGraw Propst

FUZION PRESS

ISBN 978-1-946195-10-4

My Nun and Her Husband

© 2017 Milam McGraw Propst

1st Edition

ISBN: 978-1-946195-10-4

Library of Congress Control Number: 2017941271

Cover Design: Ashley Aubitz

Layout: Brian C. Aubitz

All rights reserved. No part of this book may be reproduced or duplicated in any manner without written consent of the publisher. Reviews and brief excerpts for editorial purposes are approved.

To find additional works from the author please visit her website at:
MilamMcGrawPropst.com

Printed by
FuzionPress, 1250 E 115th Street,
Burnsville, MN, 55337 USA

612-781-2815

Dedication

Jamey, I couldn't have taken care of Kate Shilling without your support, hard work, and financial expertise. As a tiny token of my gratitude, I dedicate this book to you. Not only do I love you, but I also appreciate everything you do for me.

And, yes, I must admit, Kate did like you the best!

To Sandy Aubitz, Jackie Brown, BA Colley, and Linda Kelleher, thank you for your review of this book. Your input and/or research with helpful comments has been much appreciated.

My Nun and Her Husband

by

Milam McGraw Propst

My cellphone screamed me awake. Something was terribly wrong. I knew. I KNEW.

Unless there's an emergency, no one calls at 6 a.m. Had there been an accident? A sick grandson? A family crisis? The third jarring ring shook my entire body. I couldn't get a breath. My seven second dash to our kitchen felt as though I were running in concrete socks. I grabbed the phone.

"Yes!"

"Hello, may I speak to Milam Propst?"

"This is she." My stomach curled into knots.

"This is Melissa from Athens Regional Hospital," she began. "Do you know a Mr. Lou Shilling?"

Quivering, I croaked, "Yes."

My mind zipped from A to Z. Our friend, Kate Shilling, Lou's wife, might have died! A stroke? Her heart? She never exercises or takes proper care of herself, plus she's rather chubby. To make us laugh, Kate refers to herself as "prosperous."

In her defense, Kate's weight gain wasn't entirely her fault. Ever since Lou took over the cooking, the Shillings have eaten mostly junk food, pizza, in particular. One large pizza, with everything but onions, lasted the two of them for several meals.

My husband, Jamey, and I would move Lou into a retirement home near us in Atlanta. I envisioned the brilliant Ph.D. giving lectures to his fellow residents on photography or historic research. He might even again practice psychology.

"Lou is a very young eighty-six," I assured myself.

"Please, Melissa, please put Mr. Shilling on the phone."

I tried to calm my voice as I attempted to come up with words of encouragement for this man, a man, who absolutely adores his wife. Two peas in a pod, the Shillings never needed friends, or neighbors, or relationships of any kind. Each completed the other's world. For nearly twenty years, Jamey and I had been the single exception. We were allowed into their exclusive circle, yes, but only on their terms.

"No, ma'am, I'm afraid you don't understand. It's Mrs. Shilling, who needs you."

Kate Is Slipping

Three weeks earlier, Jamey and I were visiting Kate and Lou in their Athens home. I took Lou aside.

"I'm really worried about Kate. She's gotten worse just in the last month."

Lou came very close to scolding me. "Kate is a bit forgetful," he asserted. "It's age related dementia."

"But what if, God forbid, something were to happen to you?"

"Don't worry, Milam, I will always be here for my Kate." He hugged me.

I believed Lou, because I desperately needed to believe him. One of my worst nightmares would be having responsibility for the ninety-year-old former nun.

Jamey and I dressed, jumped in the car, and headed to Athens. I don't remember anything about the hour's drive. There was no conversation, no plan. We understood we had to get to Kate and fast. I was too overwhelmed to utter a single prayer.

We found a space in the parking deck and rushed inside. The woman at the main desk paged Melissa. The caring young social worker greeted us warmly saying, "I'm so relieved I could reach you. Mrs. Shilling carefully spelled out M-i-l-a-m P-r-o-p-s-t for me, so I was able to find your number in the White Pages."

I wondered why no one noticed our "in case of emergency" contact information on the Shillings' refrigerator. Thankfully, mine is an unusual name. I shudder to think what might have happened had I been a Mary Smith.

As we walked toward the waiting room, Melissa explained, "Mr. Shilling has suffered a massive heart attack."

Jamey was dumbstruck. My own heart broke into a thousand pieces.

There sat Kate Shilling, bewildered and lost. She looked more like a fearful child than Sister Thomas Margaret, C.S.J., circa: 1959-1963, the smart and challenging English teacher at St. Pius X Catholic High School in Atlanta. While many students either revered or feared the diminutive nun, I rather liked her.

It was the first time we'd seen Kate without her curly gray wig. She was wearing her University of Georgia baseball cap. A wispy, white pony tail trickled onto her shoulder.

"Jamey and I are here."

"Where's Lou?" she whispered from deep down inside her heavy fog.

"May we take her to him?"

"Yes, of course."

Accompanied by Melissa, we went to Lou's bedside in intensive care. Another shock. The charming, handsome man of letters was hooked up to all matter of tubes. His mouth hung open. Medical machines hummed in the background.

"This is grim," said Jamey. He was shaking. I almost vomited. Kate stood tightly clutching my hand with absolutely no expression on her face.

Two days later, Kate gave permission to have the man, who was everything to her, taken off life support.

"That's not my Lou," she replied to the attending physician. "My Lou is in Heaven."

A Bit of Background

The two met *sometime during the 1960's (*neither ever confirmed the year). At the time, she was a Sister of St. Joseph; he was a Marist priest.

Once they found each other, they struggled mightily to remain faithful to their religious vows. After all, Kate had been a nun for twenty-two and a half years. She'd joined her order at the tender age of seventeen.

In an effort to distance themselves from one another, Father Shilling transferred to Catholic University in Washington, D.C., while Sister Thomas Margaret remained in Atlanta at St. Pius. There she taught me, Linda Euart, Betty Ann Putnam, Sandy James, Jack Millkey, Flo Walsh, Tom Hughes, Kathleen Gegan, Hugh O'Donnell, Denny Bishop, John Gegan, Tommy Almon, Rita Ann Lehner, Janet Lancaster, and countless others. Thanks to the talented nun's excellent skills and open-mindedness, I propose that we, her students, were better educated in English and journalism than were a majority of our peers.

Struggle as they did to remain apart, Kate and Lou's love for one another proved too powerful a force.

It was Kate's father, who became the catalyst. He encouraged his daughter saying, "Kate, you are never as happy as when you are with Lou Shilling. You simply must do something about this!"

"You're right, Pop."

Fortified by her intuitive father's support, Kate immediately wrote to Lou. So connected were their souls, even in those early years, Lou had written to her on the very same day.

"Our letters crossed in the mail!" Kate beamed.

Lou winked at his wife. Taking his hand in hers, she leaned closer to him. I felt like an intruder!

The two would eventually exchange their religious vocations for a forty-something-year marriage.

This book is but a glimpse at their story. Some of which, they requested I write; some of which, I decided to write anyway.

Back to the Present

Kate's debilitating dementia turned out to be something of a blessing. Her failing memory provided the only way she could endure the unbearable loss of Lou.

As soon as her husband was taken off life-maintaining machines, Kate turned to Jamey and asked, "Are we going to get our pizza now?"

I was speechless.

He replied, "Sure, Kate. Let's go."

We picked up pizza and drove to the modest house the Shillings proudly named *The Homestead*. Lou's car was parked in the garage. Maybe, just maybe, he'd be inside, and this was but a horrible dream. Lou wasn't inside. The nightmare continued.

Kate only thought she was hungry. For days on end, my little nun would eat only a bite or two, if that much. This, even after Jamey dutifully grinded her meal to mush to accommodate the new widow's mouth of *missing teeth.

*Kate didn't believe in dentists, never trusted them. Eight years prior, after she'd suffered through days of intense pain, Lou insisted on taking her to a dentist. The doctor immediately sent his patient to the hospital and arranged for emergency oral surgery. Traumatic, painful, and humiliating for Kate, the surgeon removed her teeth.

The Shillings went through the entire ordeal without telling us.

For years Kate had been in the habit of calling me several times a week.

"Good morning," she'd begin cheerfully, then inquire about Jamey and me, about our family, and always, about my work. I'd not heard from her in days when Lou finally replied to my increasingly frantic phone messages.

"Kate's been a bit under the weather. That's all," he explained.

"What's wrong with her, Lou?"

"Don't you worry, Milam, just some dental work. She'll be fine."

"Dental work? What can I do to help?"

"We'll call you when she feels more like talking. Goodbye."

Another week passed before I heard from Kate. True to form, she downplayed the whole episode. "I'm doing great," she insisted. "How's the editing coming on your new book?"

Kate harbored the same aversion toward all medical people. She eventually admitted to not having seen a doctor, other than the horrid dentist, in seventy years. To repeat, that's seventy years without a single visit to a physician! Given that fact, Kate managed to remain amazingly healthy.

Throughout the traumatic days following Lou's death, I'd sit with Kate and explain over and over again that her beloved husband was gone. The news always came as a complete shock to her.

She'd hear Jamey moving about in their office.

"Lou, please come in here with us."

"Kate, Lou has passed away . . ."

I also took care of the Shillings' dog, Tallee. Eighty-six pounds of endearing yellow lab, she stood sentry by the door to the garage and awaited her master's return. Because Jamey was frequently going in and out tidying up the property and searching for important paper work, Tallee perked up any time the door opened. Whenever Jamey, not Lou appeared, the pitiful pup would hang her head and wail.

Loyal to a fault, Tallee never ventured far from the Shillings' sight. Totally devoted to the couple, she generally placed herself either between their matching recliners in the living room or at their feet under the umbrella table on the patio.

One morning I decided to take Tallee for a walk, her first ever! According to both Lou and Kate, she'd never once been in their front yard. "Too dangerous," they alleged. "She might run off."

As we ambled down the sidewalk, I thought about Neil Armstrong's historic first steps onto the moon. With its sounds, scents, and sights, Maple Forge Drive, like the moon, opened a new world for Tallee. The curious pooch enthusiastically inspected each bush and every mailbox along the way. Our daily outings offered a pleasant diversion for her and for me.

As time permitted, I began making random notes. At first, I couldn't decide whether or not to chronical the early details. I eventually decided to do so before I forgot everything. Dealing with a high level of stress puts most people into a robotic, sleepwalking mode, myself included. As a writer, I knew I should keep a record.

Most importantly, I was beginning to feel God's arms around me as He sent angel after angel to join Jamey and me in looking after Kate. Angels, angels like Melissa at Athens Regional, started to fall into place.

While I ministered to Kate and Tallee, Jamey was reviewing the Shillings' financial situation. It was a given that I'd have to find assistance for the widow and her portly pup. Even though that was going to be expensive, I thumbed through the list of home health agencies Melissa provided.

Advance Care: enter the next two angels. LaShayla was the efficient contact person, while Bernice, whom I nicknamed "B-nice," was a perfect companion for Kate. She was caring, patient, and resourceful. We got lucky. From the start, Kate and Bernice hit it off beautifully.

"Mrs. Shilling," said B-nice, "everything will work out fine. You'll see."

I prayed the optimistic caregiver was right. But how could she be? Kate was in a terrible predicament. Or, as the Lou's widow remarked during one rare moment of clarity, "I'm in quite a pickle, aren't I?"

Indeed, she was.

Bernice and I listened attentively as Kate repeated her one vivid memory, "Lou turned his head to the side and never uttered another word."

Bernice patted her hand.

Kate didn't remember Lou's calling 911. She thought she'd dialed the number herself, but the poor woman couldn't distinguish between their cellphone and the television clicker. Kate had no memory whatsoever of their ambulance ride to the emergency room or even of Lou's death two days later.

Kate would write on her notepad, "Lou died at 5:30 p.m. on September 14."

A minute passed. Still clutching her pad, she'd ask, "Where's Lou?"

One awful morning Kate took a tumble. Jamey and I were frantic. We helped her onto her feet and back into her chair.

"I'm all right."

We wanted to believe her. I certainly couldn't talk her into seeing a doctor.

"Please let us know the next time you want to get up!"

I contacted LaShayla and engaged Advance Care for twenty-four hours a day, seven days a week. I began looking into assisted living facilities, only to discover Kate would have to submit to a physician's examination to be considered for admittance. Dementia notwithstanding, it would have been easier on her to earn her third Master's degree.

Our next hurdle was the mandatory TB skin test. I contacted local clinics, Walgreens, and several physicians, including Lou's own trusted doctor. I assumed, because Kate always accompanied her husband to his checkups, the doctor's office staff might be kind enough to assist us. It's been many months now and their mean-spirited refusal to help continues to eat a hole in me!

I shared my growing anxiety with Bernice.

"Sugar, why didn't you ask me in the first place?" she chided.

Bernice knew of a public health facility where the TB test could be administered. When the time came, she went with us.

The obstacle would have been a total game changer had it not been for Bernice. B-nice was both an angel and a gem.

Ice Water

I sat straight up in our bed. The realization washed over me like a bucket full of ice cold water. Kate had absolutely no support except for us. Jamey and I were in charge of the lady, of her care, of her finances, of her future. Holy crap.

"Lou Shilling, what should Jamey and I DO?" I implored with my hands lifted toward the dark ceiling.

Lou didn't answer.

Surely Kate had someone in addition to Jamey and me?

Tom Small, Kate's only sibling, had been murdered in 1954. Yes, I typed *murdered*. We knew nothing about his death other than he was fatally shot through the window of an Atlanta restaurant.

At least, we knew nothing until a month before this book went to press. Sandy James Aubitz, a St. Pius alum and lifelong friend, discovered an article about Kate's brother in a Georgia Tech alumni publication. (*In 1941, after three years at Tech, Tom left school to serve in the U.S. Army. After the war, the courageous soldier returned to graduate in the Class of 1947).

According to the story, Tom was shot by an escaped convict. The murderer was said to be aiming at another customer and escaped in a taxi cab.

Horrors! I cannot imagine. It was tragic enough for the Smalls to lose Tom at the young age of thirty-five. But after surviving WWII, he was lost to his family in such a senseless and violent manner.

Little wonder Tom's death was a topic Kate and Lou avoided discussing. Her conversations about her older brother were confined to their idyllic childhood and to their parents, who loved them dearly. She liked to reminisce about a Boston Terrier named Jiggs and about playing football with Tom and their friends in their close knit neighborhood near E. Rivers School in Atlanta.

She often quoted Tom's teasing her, "Kate, you are the most un-nunny nun in the world!"

Kate's worst memory was that she was denied permission by the Sisters of St. Joseph to be present at Tom's funeral.

"You weren't allowed to attend your own brother's funeral?" I gasped.

She and Lou locked eyes. The two always acted, thought, spoke, and believed as a single person. As if a black mask suddenly covered her face, Kate said not another word. The same darkness enveloped her husband.

"Little wonder you left the convent," said Jamey.

Lou rose to his feet, clapped his hands together, and said, "Who's ready to go to lunch?"

Lou does have a younger sister named Trudy, who lives in Williamsburg, Virginia, with her husband Tommy. Unfortunately, for the last thirty to forty years, Kate and Lou had seen little of Trudy and Tommy. Once was in 2002, before the Shillings moved from Brevard, North Carolina, to Athens, Georgia.

Trudy made another attempt to reconnect with her brother and his wife. She came alone explaining that her husband was not in optimum health. I do recall Kate's being extremely apprehensive about entertaining a house guest. To my knowledge, the Shillings had not hosted an overnight visitor in decades. Trudy thoughtfully stayed in a nearby hotel.

Jamey and I volunteered to pick up Lou's sister at the Atlanta airport. Along the way to Athens, we stopped for a get acquainted lunch, which opened the door to our friendship.

We've exchanged occasional e-mails and annual Christmas cards ever since. I frequently shared Trudy's news with the Shillings. Because they talked on the phone only on birthdays and holidays, Kate and Lou seemed to enjoy my updates.

Upon our arrival in Athens, Kate and Lou walked outside to welcome Trudy. I snapped a photo of Trudy and Lou standing together in front of *The Homestead.* Checking out the picture, Lou commented, "Trudy, I never realized we looked so much alike!"

*In a recent email to Trudy, I reminded her of the visit. She saw it as a great success, saying Kate and Lou were excellent hosts.

I cannot imagine how uncomfortable our relationship with Trudy might have been following Lou's death, had we not met one another under such pleasant circumstances. I like Lou's sister very much. We both do. Not knowing the reason surrounding their distanced relationship, I'll simply comment, as I've told Trudy, "It was the Shillings' loss."

One of the hardest calls I've ever had to make was telling Trudy about Lou's death.

"But Lou's so healthy!" she uttered in disbelief.

"I know, Trudy. We always assumed Lou would outlive Kate."

Trudy offered to come to help out, but her health prohibited her from doing so. To this day, her emotional support is important to me.

The only other relative I can mention is Kate and Lou's son, Andy. Even as I write his name, I question whether or not I should include this story. What we know is very, very limited, not a surprise given how guarded the Shillings have always been.

The Shillings adopted Andy sometime during the early seventies. A cute fellow, he had curly, flaming red hair and was the delight of their lives for six years.

In 1970, after Lou earned his Ph.D., he accepted a teaching job at Clark Atlanta University. Thrilled as they could be, the Shillings purchased a home, moved, and enjoyed their adorable little boy. When Lou's father passed away, his mother, Isabell, came to live with her son and Kate. From what I understand, Andy got along famously with his grandmother.

Texas Women's College in Denton contacted Lou in 1975 to offer him a position, which included a raise in salary. The Shillings accepted. Isabell, who was becoming homesick for Virginia, decided to return to Williamsburg. That summer the

Shillings drove across country looking forward to a new adventure. Once in Denton, Andy entered elementary school and Kate tutored in the afternoons. Lou taught at the college from 1976-1983, prior to going into private practice.

Kate confided in us that their son's personality changed drastically during his first grade year. Andy became increasingly angry, often exhibiting violent behavior and acting out. Even though their child was raised by liberal and accepting parents, he was extremely uneasy and suspicious around both Jews and black people.

The situation worsened all throughout their son's school years.

"It was as if our Andy were turning into a Nazi!" lamented Kate.

"A psychologist myself," added Lou, "I was completely baffled by his erratic behavior."

The Shillings remained devoted to one another, and, for as long as they could, to their family of three. However, when Andy turned sixteen, he suddenly announced his plans to leave home. With seemingly no reason they could think of, the troubled teenager wanted to move to Guam.

"Guam, did you say?"

"Yes, I had a connection with a former colleague. The man happened to be on assignment in Guam," said Lou. "He generously offered living quarters to Andy."

"What happened next?" I urged.

Kate and Lou again looked to one another.

Lou answered haltingly, "We really don't know. Andy got into a fight in a bar and injured his hand. After a trip to the hospital, he called us asking for money to pay his doctor bills. Of course, I wired him the cash."

"It was the very last time we heard from our son," said Kate. Her eyes glazed over.

Lou corrected her. "Remember the man who called me from Florida offering information about Andy?"

She nodded. They sighed in tandem. The call turned out to be nothing but a cruel scam for money.

Little wonder the Shillings became suspicious of people. Sometimes I question what it was about Jamey and me they felt they could trust.

The bottom line: with no family or close friends, Kate Shilling's well-being rested firmly upon our shoulders.

Mountain Retreat

In 1989, two years after Andy's departure, Lou retired and the Shillings found solace in a cozy mountaintop cottage in Brevard. They had loved the mountains ever since a vacation trip to Asheville decades prior. Still a nun and a priest at the time, Kate insisted they were properly chaperoned by her parents!

"We had two cabins," she explained. "One was for the girls and one was for the men."

Lou taught briefly at Western Carolina, while Kate took care of Carla, a mixed breed black lab. Throughout their marriage, the Shillings were never without a dog.

In addition to Carla, Kate raised fancy guppies in four large tanks in their guest bedroom. One morning she called me to request we deliver a new pair of fish to her. I waited for the punchline to her joke.

"I looked on the internet," she continued. "There's a pet shop on Peachtree Street which carries the kind I want."

No punchline followed.

I never could say "no" to my teacher. We purchased the guppies a couple of hours before heading out for Brevard. I feared for the lives of those fragile sea creatures as they sloshed about in their cardboard containers. The more mountain curves, the more they sloshed. Would brain damage ensue? If so, how could one tell?

"Thank you!" said Kate as she introduced the guppies to their tank-mates. Her smile was gratitude enough. The guppies adjusted to their surroundings without noticeable developmental problems.

The Shillings frequently traveled throughout the North Carolina mountains and along the Blue Ridge Parkway. Lou took pleasure in his hobby of taking photographs of fall foliage, waterfalls, winter scenery, wild flowers and shrubbery, birds, deer, and stunning mountain vistas. Back home in their comfy retreat, Kate penned marvelous poems to compliment her husband's photographs. We treasure four volumes of their photographic and poetic work as a testament to their talents.

The two of them also began work on what was to become an all-consuming passion of researching the lives of Emily Dickenson and of her mentor, Thomas Wentworth Higginson. Kate felt a deep kinship with Emily, while Lou was drawn to

Thomas. Together they wrote two comprehensive academic biographies; hers is entitled *Emily's Laughter* and his is *Unity Amid Variety*.

The Shillings were never quite aggressive enough to actively pursue a publisher but remained completely satisfied with their end products. They made several copies of each book for themselves, for us, and for future readers.

I will end this chapter with a rather endearing commentary about Kate and Lou and their style of dress. The two were strictly casual with Kate consistently dressed in her warmup pants and Lou in his jeans. The color of their tops always, always matched! If Kate wore blue, green, or yellow, Lou followed suit. Depending on the season, they each donned red and black for UGA or Falcons football. Of course, both wore red on Valentine's Day and Christmas.

Domingo and More Angels Appear

I made a note in my records: "Jamey and I continue to have our hands full. Lord, help us."

As home healthcare accelerated, people would be coming and going around the clock.

Given Kate and Lou's reclusiveness, company was a rarity, so I decided to alert the neighbors. After no one answered on their left, I scribbled a note to them and walked over to the house on the right. I knocked. I knocked again.

Looking very fearful, a Hispanic man finally answered. The fretful look on my face added to his apprehension.

"I'm Domingo. I am an American citizen!"

"Congratulations," I replied with a grin. "I'm Milam Propst, also a citizen."

Deciding I wasn't "the law," Domingo relaxed. I told him about Lou's passing and explained about Kate's sitters.

"I never saw the lady, only the man."

Then to my surprise, Domingo burst into tears. In perfect English, he said, "Lou was his name? He died? Oh no, oh no!"

"I'm sorry to tell you this."

"Only a few days ago, I watched him cutting grass on his riding lawnmower."

"Must not have been long before his heart attack."

"Such a nice man. He always waved at me when he went to the mailbox or took out his trash, or," Domingo choked up again, "rode his mower."

By our conversation's end, Domingo and I were hugging one another. He asked if he might go with me to call on Lou's wife. I saw his as a very thoughtful gesture and agreed to introduce him. Entering the Shillings' house, the gentle neighbor first petted Tallee. He then got down on his knees in front of Kate.

"I'm very sorry for your loss."

Domingo stayed only a few minutes but his visit was quite uplifting.

Upon leaving, he said, "I used to work at a hospital in Winston Salem. I'd like to help, if you'll allow me."

The caring neighbor did help. He checked on Kate every evening. I lost count of the number of angels the Lord was sending our way. With competent people taking care of my nun, I was free to visit assisted living homes in Atlanta. At the suggestion of our friend, Pam Weeks, I went to Hollander Senior Living.

Without my friends, Pam, Linda, BA, Jackie, Claire, Mary and Marvin, Judy, Beverly, and Helen, I could not have survived. Bless them for their prayers and encouragement and for their worn out ears from listening to me. Bless Trudy for her understanding emails and for the gorgeous orchid she and Tommy sent the end of a particularly unsettling day. Bless our children, who texted and encouraged me. Obviously, I'm someone who needs a great deal of support.

Where was I? Oh yes, I stumbled into the Hollander office speaking like a combination of an auctioneer and Daffy Duck. Sheila offered me a cup of coffee.

"Thanks, but no more caffeine for me today. As it is, I can hardly steer my car!"

The newest angel let me rant until I gathered myself. I liked Sheila, her facility, and her staff. Unfortunately, the monthly cost was more than we could afford.

"I also run Hollander Senior Living in Monroe," offered Sheila. "It's larger, newer, and cheaper. By the way, off the screen porch, there's a pond with ducks."

Praise BE, ducks even! I had no idea if Kate liked ducks or not, but I do. The Good Lord was thoughtfully sending some darling ducks our way.

The next day on our way to Kate's, Jamey and I stopped in Monroe. As we entered the front door of Hollander, a warm, light-filled lobby beckoned us to come inside. Marie, our next angel, greeted us with a big smile and showed us to the living room and dining area. Shelia held out her arms as she walked from her office. As we stood together on the screen porch, I spotted the aforementioned ducks. Good smells wafted from the kitchen. A lovely apartment, nice staff, and the place was as clean as it could be. We immediately began the intake process.

A couple of hours later, we arrived at *The Homestead*.

Bernice came through the garage to greet us. "No more falls," she announced.

"Lou!" Kate exclaimed.

"No, Kate, it's only us."

I reminded Kate her husband was gone. Always the educator, Kate made a note on her pad. "Lou died at 5:30 p.m. on September 14, 2015."

Bernice took me aside.

"Mrs. Shilling was fussing this morning. She said, 'Milam is wrong. My Lou has been dead a very long time.'"

While we visited, Jamey continued to dig through Lou's filing system. Even though his files were organized, Lou's computer passwords were undiscernible. The Shillings were paranoid about people knowing their business and always feared their computers might be hacked. At one point, Kate even stopped emailing me. For a decade plus, our emails served as the building blocks for our adult relationship.

Kate showed me her notepad. "Lou died at 5:30 p.m. on September 14, 2015."

I hugged her. "I know, Kate, this is awful. You must miss Lou terribly."

It amazed me that she wasn't curled up in a ball, weeping. I was thankful for her sweet balm of confusion.

"Lou died at 5:30 p.m. on September 14, 2015," she repeated as if to teach herself. Tallee sat patiently at her side.

Jamey suddenly leapt up from Lou's desk and charged into the living room. Tallee shuddered and rose to her feet. Had I not seen my husband's big smile, I'd have assumed there was another crisis.

"I found Kate's Medicare card, her driver's license (for ID), and her social security card!"

Jamey Propst couldn't have been more excited had he come upon a pirate's chest overflowing with gold medallions.

It goes without saying, a chest full of gold would have come in handy. Home healthcare is expensive and so is assisted living. However, faith abounds. I trusted God to provide for my nun.

Hadn't He already gifted us with a pond of ducks?

Heading Home to Hollander

September 22 was moving day. That morning Bernice and I took Kate for her TB skin test. On our way home, Kate said she wanted a hot dog from the Varsity, a spot the Shillings enjoyed during their early married years at the University of Georgia.

"Kate, while you were teaching and Lou was working on his Ph.D., how many hot dogs DID you eat?"

My attempt at levity only puzzled Kate.

"Lord, Mrs. Shilling," said Bernice, "you and your husband sure were smart!"

"A hot dog with no onions," replied Kate. "I don't like onions."

Bernice, Kate, and I sat in the kitchen as the poor widow tried to ingest her ground up hot dog. Since Lou's death, Jamey's turkey dressing was the only thing Kate seemed to enjoy. I don't know what I'd have done without Jamey's ingenuity, along with his patience, and his ability to figure out finances. That day he was taking on the back-breaking job of moving furniture. God surely blesses my husband.

"Kate, your hot dog doesn't taste as good as you remembered."

She gazed out the sliding doors to the patio. In moment of perfect clarity, Kate sighed, "I suppose this is the last time I'll sit here and look out at our lovely yard."

Bernice and I both welled up with tears.

My mind drifted back to the pleasant times Kate, Lou, and I sat around their kitchen table. After our lunches in a variety of Athens fast food spots, we always enjoyed a piece of key lime pie at home. Before having dessert, however, we would tour the Maple Forge subdivision.

Kate sat in the front seat with Lou. I'd sit in the back wishing I were their daughter.

Ever proud of their home, we'd look to see if a neighbor might have a house for sale. The Shillings conjured up the idea Jamey and I were going to move down the street from them. In fact, there was one particular two-story they frequently pointed out to me.

"Jamey could plant his vegetable garden in the side yard," remarked Lou. "He'd have perfect morning sun."

I also remembered stimulating discussions, years ago, about art, music, prose, and poetry, along with some rather heated conversations about politics. How I'd have loved auguring about current issues with them on that mournful moving day.

I truly appreciated the Shillings' interest in my family and our grandsons, Loftin and Emmett. Kate always wanted to hear how the little Propst boys were doing in school. She had a vested interest in their academic success and was thrilled when they attended Christ the King, the school from which she graduated.

Kate relished hearing about her former Pius students. She delighted in the number of future teachers she'd encouraged and saluted our many classmates who continued on to graduate schools. Kate was particularly pleased with one of her students, Hugh O'Donnell, an attorney, who champions the plight of coal miners in West Virginia.

Four years ago, Jamey had knee replacement surgery. For the next two years, Kate inquired about him nearly every day.

As time passed and she became more confused, she'd ask, "How are Jamey's feet doing?"

In the beginning, I'd correct her, "Kate, it's Jamey's knee and it's completely healed."

"Are Jamey's feet getting better?"

"His knee is perfect, Kate."

"Jamey's feet?"

"His feet are fine."

As her memory was fading away, Kate's love and concern remained a constant.

The Caravan

"We're heading out," shouted Jamey.

His sudden words jolted me back to reality.

"Good luck. Be careful."

Jamey and Domingo had loaded a U-Haul with everything we thought Kate might need in her new apartment.

"We'll come along in an hour or so," I said.

Jamey replied, "I don't know how long this might take. I'll give you a call."

"Heading out" sounded so final. It was. We'd hardly found time to mourn Lou. Now we were pushing Kate out of their house into assisted living. Second thoughts? Certainly!

When Jamey backed the rental truck up the driveway, I tried to convince myself this was the safest plan for Kate. Unfortunately, all I could do was dwell on how excited Kate and Lou were when they first moved from Brevard. As content as they had been in North Carolina, the cold winters became too challenging for them, for Lou, most especially. He worried that his beloved wife might slip and fall on the ice.

"We both dread those long winters," explained Lou. "Because we live atop the mountain, our power outages last for days on end. I have to take care of my Kate!"

I like to believe the Shillings also wanted to live closer to us. I imagined them visiting and getting to know our family and friends. It never happened. Kate and Lou remained adamant about on our coming to them.

Naturally, Kate and Lou refused our help with their move. They didn't want us to be troubled. We would have showed up anyway; but, in typical Shilling style, they didn't inform us until they were already in their new home. Both of them were completely exhausted. Neither admitted it.

"The most beautiful full moon greeted us last night," swooned Kate. "It appeared outside our bedroom window as if to say, 'Hello, Shillings two!'"

I again glanced around their kitchen and recalled a decade of exchanging Christmas presents. Their gifts for us included books from Barnes & Noble, cookies and candy, and

Lou's photographs, which he framed himself. He frequently saluted his father for teaching him the valuable skill.

"Thanks, Dad. With as many photos as I've framed, you've saved us a fortune."

Our gifts to the Shillings were as practical as a Christmas robe or socks, but more often, were as silly as a holiday tree covered with "apples for my teacher." The tree was donated to Goodwill. Continuing in the mindset of a nun and a priest, the Shillings were minimalists decades before the style became trendy.

As charter members of the Bulldog Nation, any item we brought with a University of Georgia logo was a keeper, were it matching hats, mugs, glasses, or a key ring. They also pulled for the Atlanta Falcons. After years of cheering on the Dallas Cowboys, they'd become rabid converts to the Atlanta team. We purchased Falcons hats for them, too. A perfect weekend for the Shillings occurred when both their teams won.

Our Birthday Bashes were epic in the minds of the Shillings. It provided an annual excuse to share a delicious cake from the Publix bakery.

Kate delighted in saying, "We three, Milam, Lou, and I, are Aquarians on the Zodiac calendar."

"Jamey, you're the odd man out," teased Lou, referring to my husband's June birthday.

"We love you anyway," smiled Kate.

My cellphone rang sounding like a three-alarm fire. Bernice and I sprang to our feet.

"Y'all, come on," said Jamey.

Just then, LaShayla came through the front door. "All set to go?"

"Your timing is perfect. Jamey just called. They're ready for us."

It was not perfect! I couldn't turn back the clock to our years of conversations and celebrations. It was not perfect, for I certainly couldn't slow the process of Kate's dementia. And, the least perfect thing of all, I couldn't stop Kate from losing her home. It was too late.

As the ladies walked Kate toward the front door, I thought she petted Tallee goodbye. Did she not? I truly cannot recall. Poor old dog, poor, poor, sweet Tallee. Could the pooch possibly comprehend any of what was happening to her world?

We helped Kate into Bernice's sedan. It was easier than our lifting her up into my Jeep. We loaded her wheelchair and drove off in our caravan of three.

Kate had lost Lou and now she was leaving her beloved home. Because we were taking Tallee to Atlanta, she was also losing her precious pet. Kate Shilling's life had changed forever.

Could assisted living possibly work out for her? Kate and Lou had their established routine: "early to bed, early to rise," breakfast at 5:30 a.m., midday dinner at 11 a.m., supper at 6 p.m., all with very little contact with other people. How would this already confused person possibly adjust to communal living with its schedules and rules AND with all sorts of strangers around her? On we drove. I was glad I was alone, so I could pray.

"Lou, what have I done?"

"Welcome, Kate Shilling"

The Hollander staff, led by the ever charming Sheila, welcomed Kate. While we sipped iced tea on the comfortable porch, each worker politely introduced herself or himself to Hollander's newest resident.

Kate relished the attention.

"The duchess has arrived," I teased. The scene was something out of *Downton Abbey*.

"Ready to see your new home?" invited Sheila.

We pushed Kate in her wheelchair down the long hallway to Apartment 17. Sheila opened the door.

"It looks like my living room!" exclaimed Kate.

"Nice job, Jamey and Domingo," I praised.

There were Kate's tables and lamps, her comfy blue recliner, her prized clock and music box, her bookcases, her rocking chair, and her television. Jamey even thoughtfully made up her bed.

As Kate looked around, my husband pulled me aside. "Domingo dropped the TV. Not sure it will work."

I had to laugh.

Bernice offered to stay with Kate for the first night or two. How like B-nice to do that!

Totally exhausted, Jamey and I thanked Bernice profusely and said goodbye to Sheila and her staff. *I hope I remembered to thank them for Kate's lovely welcome.

We both hugged Kate, who didn't react in the least to our leaving. I felt encouraged.

"Long damn day, Baby Doll," said Jamey.

"Thank goodness the move is over."

Jamey dropped off the U-Haul truck and took Domingo home.

Epic Meltdown

We met back at *The Homestead* and loaded the pitiful Tallee into the backseat of Jamey's car. "It's going to be all right, sweet puppy," I said rubbing her ears.

Tallee's soulful brown eyes looked into mine as if she were asking, "Where are my people?"

"See you at home," said Jamey.

"Thank you so much for your hard work."

"You're welcome, Baby Doll. Be careful."

"You, too."

I walked back inside the Shillings' house. Big mistake.

With Kate's furniture gone, I realized the carpet was ankle-deep in Tallee's fur.

"Lou, could you not occasionally run the vacuum?"

I'd expected to be saddened by the home's emptiness, but I was more shocked than anything else. I slammed the front door, locked up, and got into my Jeep. I drove toward Jefferson

Highway, the route Lou had discovered for me. He used to worry about the heavy traffic and frequent red lights on Highway 316.

"Lou, you promised, 'I will always be here for my Kate.' Where the heck were you today when we had to move your poor wife out of your home? And Tallee, too!"

Lou had become father-like to me, but that didn't stop me from becoming increasingly angry. I turned onto the highway. I cannot speak for Jamey, but had Lou not already been dead, I might have killed him.

My speedometer read, "70 MPH." I slowed down.

"Lou, did you not know you had a heart condition?"

I wanted to believe his massive heart attack came out of the blue, but we'd already found several unpaid bills from a cardiologist.

As though my Jeep had a mind of its own, it sped up again.

"Lou, your house is a complete mess. There are thick layers of dust covering everything. We had to clean each book, painting, lamp, and piece of furniture we took to Hollander."

80 MPH.

"Your bathrooms are toxic! Kate's looks as though a baby powder bomb exploded in there."

85 MPH.

Again I applied the brakes. Lucky for me, there was no policeman around. Lou had warned me about the speed trap in Arcade. What a fatherly thing for him to do.

My composure didn't last long.

"About the leak you told us 'miraculously fixed itself'? Wrong! Do you remember your favorite photo of you and Kate, the one which held the place of honor on your mantel? Sorry to tell you, but it's ruined. Water from the *miracle* roof repair got in between your picture and the glass. When I tried to free it, you and Kate fell to pieces."

I, too, was falling to pieces. Almost out of gas, I stopped to fill my tank and buy a diet Dr. Pepper.

"Pull yourself together, Milam." I prayed. I bought a pack of cheese crackers. Like Kate, I wasn't hungry for my Varsity hot dog either. More prayer.

As I sat in the service station parking lot, it became crystal clear to me. I wasn't mad about his messy house. I was furious at Lou for dying.

He and Kate were family to me. As weird as it is to admit, they were mine, all mine. They filled the big void left by Jamey's parents and by my own. The Shillings had become parents, parents, who not only offered stimulating conversations, but who also gave me their unconditional love and understanding. They never once judged me. In some ways, Kate seemed to know me better than I knew myself. The loss was unbearable. Once again I was orphaned.

Worse still, this orphan and her husband were left with a ninety-year-old dependent!

Tears running down my cheeks, I said, "Lord, help us. Please."

I took a deep breath. "Pull yourself, Milam."

I ate the last cheese cracker, turned back onto the highway, and headed toward the interstate with a trace of composure. At least, I was no longer a danger to other drivers.

50 MPH.

"I'm sorry, Lou, forgive me. I'm completely worn out physically and emotionally. We both are. Jamey and I are worried about everything, but we will be here for your Kate. We will do our best."

60 MPH.

I suppose you and Kate were so preoccupied with your creative efforts, you had no time for housework."

I chugged what was left of my soft drink.

Maybe the Shillings had made the better choice after all. Weren't *Emily's Laughter* and the Higginson book more important than vacuuming and cleaning bathrooms? After the dust was long gone, their work would endure.

"Lou, were you and Kate too involved with one another to pay attention to much of anything else?"

That's the truth of it. The Shillings had chosen a higher path. Other couples should be as consumed by their own relationships. I was learning yet another lesson from a dead man and his very confused wife.

65 MPH.

Flannery O'Connor

I had made an about-face. Prayer? Yes, and the snack helped.

Kept at a slower pace by the growing evening traffic, I decided to recall one of my favorite Kate stories. It's about the former Sister Thomas Margaret and Flannery O'Connor. I love, simply love that our English teacher was acquainted with the renowned Southern author.

Kate was guarded about the subject, so it wasn't easy to get her to discuss their relationship. As with most personal topics, Kate was reluctant to talk about her past, including her encounters with Flannery.

Lou was in the backyard with his camera, so I pushed Kate just enough to get her to share the following memory.

As a young nun, Sister Thomas Margaret taught at Sacred Heart School in Milledgeville. She often saw Flannery and her mother, Regina, at the daily Mass in Sacred Heart Church.

"It was unsettling to watch Flannery struggle with those crutches," she began.

"How horrible for her to suffer from Lupus."

Kate shook her head. "The same debilitating illness which took her father."

"She and Regina knew exactly what was coming," I replied. "So sad."

Lou charged into the room, "Got it!"

He produced a close-up photograph of a cardinal sitting on their birdfeeder. "Took me forever to get this shot." he bragged showing us his camera. "Worth my patience, I'd say."

I applauded.

Kate looked my way, "Doesn't my Lou take the most wonderful photos?"

"He does. Should we be expecting a framed red cardinal for Christmas?"

"That's a given," said Lou.

"Too bad it's not a peacock," commented Kate. "We were just talking about Flannery. She actually enjoyed those loud, nasty birds!"

"Shall we drive to Andalusia?" quipped Lou. "It should be easier for me to capture a picture of a slow moving peacock than one of our flighty cardinal."

"*Flighty* cardinal! Good one, Lou."

I enjoyed their ongoing banter. The Shillings never seemed to run out of things to say to one another. She absolutely delighted in his jokes.

Kate cleared her throat signaling she was ready to continue our conversation. I sat up straight as if in my desk at St. Pius. Old habits die hard.

"At the end of World War II, Flannery's mother took in a family of Polish immigrants," Kate continued. "The husband, who'd worked his own farmland in Poland, would help her run Andalusia."

"Flannery's novella, *The Displaced Person*."

"Correct. You write what you know," taught Kate. "Flannery was no exception."

I nodded in agreement.

"The family's young children were in my class at Sacred Heart and were very well behaved."

"Your St. Pius students were well behaved, too; or you'd send them out to stand in the hall."

"Them, Milam? YOU were sent out to the hall."

"Never! Listen to her, Lou. For once, your wife is wrong!"

"Humph."

I winked at Lou.

Kate again cleared her throat to get us back on track.

"You were saying?" I encouraged.

Kate adjusted her chair and leaned my way.

"One afternoon Flannery and Regina came by our convent. To show us their appreciation for our teaching the immigrants' children, they presented us with a large, freshly killed and dressed goose for Christmas dinner. We thanked them, of course."

"Of course."

"As they were leaving, I warned Flannery, 'You'd best not write anything about me in one of your short stories. I'll get you for that!'"

"Did she?"

"No! Haven't you read her work?"

I swallowed hard. "I thought so."

"Am I in there anywhere?"

"Guess not."

"End of story," she said with a firm shake of her head.

Over the years, I've shared information about Kate and Lou with fellow St. Pius alums. Many of her former students credit Sister Thomas Margaret with being one of their finest teachers. Unfortunately, Kate permitted me to bring only two to see her. The first was Betty Ann Putnam Colley.

BA was visiting in Atlanta, so, with the Shillings' approval, I drove her to Athens. Our teacher had an ulterior motive. She wanted to apologize to BA for making her the business manager of *The Golden Lines*, our award-winning high school newspaper. She feared, which was possibly true, her decision might have squelched her student's writing talent.

Our visit was a pleasant one. The Shillings became totally engaged with BA as they asked questions about her family and her career. Our old teacher's concerns were put to rest when BA talked glowingly about becoming a physical therapist. Kate realized she'd made the right decision after all.

On our way back to Atlanta, BA commented, "It felt pretty weird talking to Sister Thomas Margaret and her HUSBAND."

"Try to think of her as Kate."

"It's still bizarre."

"I know, BA. What started out as simple curiosity on my part morphed into my becoming a member of their family."

"I repeat," she said. "It's just plain weird!"

Once Kate was settled into Hollander, she became more open to having company. The second visitor from the Class of 1963 was Linda Euart Kelleher, another member of our newspaper staff. Linda thoughtfully brought Kate a pen and matching tablet with a hard back, which made it easier for her to hold. Linda also gave our teacher a tabletop Christmas tree, which we decorated with Kate's supervision. We earned her thumbs up.

John Harrison Gegan (now John Harrison) is another one of Sister's appreciative students. He wanted to salute Kate in a unique manner, so, after touring Andalusia with his wife, Jodie, John purchased a lovely watercolor print of the O'Connor home.

He and Jodie had the piece framed and presented it to the library at St. Pius with a plaque which reads:

In honor of Sister Thomas Margaret, C.S.J. Given to the Flannery O'Connor Library, Saint Pius X High School, Atlanta, Georgia, on behalf of the Senior Honors English Class of 1963, John McCaslin MacGeoghegan Harrison

I was thrilled for Kate. Herself? Not so. I pleaded with her to write John a thank you note. She refused. I almost wrote one myself, except I could never have duplicated her excellent penmanship. I even asked Lou to encourage his wife to respond to the gesture.

"Lou, John has gone to so much trouble and expense to honor Kate. It's not like her to offend anyone."

"I'm sorry, Milam. It's not going to happen."

As I think back, Kate's obstinacy marked the early stages of her oncoming dementia.

When I talked with John, he seemed to understand, saying he'd created his tribute without any expectations.

On behalf of Sister Thomas Margaret, John, we thank you.

He even shared an interesting morsel for this book.

"Prior to my transferring to St. Pius, Father Shilling was my geometry instructor at Marist. As I recall," John added, "his classes were pretty intense!"

I wasn't surprised.

So on I write. It is not the famous Flannery O'Connor, but I, a former newspaper reporter and storyteller, who is penning this narrative. The difference? The Shillings gave me the assignment. Flannery passed away in 1964, but I like to believe Kate and Lou would have selected me anyway.

"You better not begin writing our story until after we're gone," instructed Kate. True to form, Lou agreed wholeheartedly with his wife.

Tallee, the Rest of the Story

By the time I arrived home the evening of Kate's move to Hollander, Jamey had settled Tallee in, checked his emails, and was on the phone ordering Chinese food.

Our big black dog, Bella, greeted me at the door with an expression of total dismay. Poor girl! She'd been an "only dog" for almost fourteen years.

"Bella, this is temporary, I promise."

Her mouth opened slightly making her appear to smile.

Hanging up the phone, Jamey asked why it had taken me so long to get home.

"I almost called you."

"I was talking to Lou."

"Huh?"

"Traffic."

Sometimes, it's a good thing my husband doesn't hear everything I say. It might scare him.

I fed the dogs and attempted to walk them as a pair. Neither cooperated, so I dropped off Tallee and took Bella for a solo stroll. She relaxed a little bit, as did I. Tomorrow would have to be better.

My favorite Tallee story involves a butterfly.

Every day at sunrise, weather permitting, Tallee sat with the Shillings on their patio. Kate and Lou enjoyed their morning coffee and doled out bits of toast to her or, on occasion, a gooey bite of sweet roll. One such pristine morning, Tallee was sunning herself near the bluebird house, when a butterfly flited over the back fence and into her territory. Lou quickly leapt up to shoo it away, but he wasn't fast enough. The pup opened her mouth, captured the butterfly, and trotted toward the couple as they watched in horror.

"Lou!"

"Tallee, stop!"

Unfazed by their dramatic reaction, Tallee gently released her captive as if to say, "Calm down, everyone. I have a gift for you."

Of the eight or nine dogs the Shillings have held dear, Kate always insisted Tallee was the sweetest and the smartest.

She often recounted the charming story of Tallee and her butterfly.

"She understands every word we say. Sometimes we have to spell out our messages to one another," said Kate.

"Especially," added Lou with a laugh, "if our conversation involves taking her to the vet."

I tried to hold on to positive images of Tallee, because our first few days of having her with us presented quite a challenge. While Bella became increasingly distraught, Tallee howled, panted, and paced. In defense of the dog, she had watched her lifeless master wheeled out on a gurney and stood by helplessly as Bernice and Domingo lifted Kate off the floor following yet another fall. She was then kidnapped to Atlanta for an unknown future with another aged pooch, a diet, and twice daily walks.

An army of animal lovers signed on to help us find Tallee a good home. Included were lab rescue people, our veterinarian's staff, caring neighbors, and concerned friends.

Thus far we'd all struck out. No one wanted to adopt an elderly, almost ninety-pound pooch. And to make matters worse, Tallee forgot she was housebroken. Our home was getting nastier by the hour.

Kate used to brag, "Tallee is like a cat. She grooms herself. In all these years, we've only bathed her once."

Ugh.

Like the Shillings and their housekeeping, Tallee's self-cleaning skills left much to be desired. The dog absolutely reeked. I asked Jamey to give her a long overdue bath, to which he quickly agreed.

A few minutes later, my husband bounded up the basement stairs shouting, "The damn dog has ringworm!"

Jamey Propst obsesses about ringworm. It comes from growing up in the country. The skin malady creeps me out, too, and I'm a city girl. I imagined our whole family, including Bella, becoming as bald as bowling balls. I called Wieuca Animal Clinic as soon as it opened and begged for an appointment.

"You can come in at 11:30," offered the receptionist.

"Is right NOW too soon?" Not giving her a chance to reply, I announced, "We're on our way!"

I managed to lift the dog into my Jeep and headed to our vet. Upon checking Tallee, they assured me she did not have ringworm, only infected hot spots, along with an ear infection. They asked to keep her for several hours for a complete checkup, an ear cleaning, and a medical bath with possible fur shaving. I couldn't say yes fast enough. I seized on the opportunity to visit Kate without concern for Tallee and our angst-ridden Bella.

Sheila was right. Kate Shilling was already improving due to healthier meals and the social stimulation at Hollander. My nun's brain back in gear, she had me unpacking her books and hanging pictures, moving her chair away from the glare of the French doors, and making notes of items for me to bring next visit. Topping her list was her favorite brand of baby powder. Hopefully, the staff would be able to hold powder buildup to a minimum.

Another angel, Marvin the maintenance man, stopped by Kate's apartment to install her new television, the one we bought to replace the set Domingo dropped. That crisis took a positive turn as Kate delighted in receiving her house warming present.

I showed Marvin a picture of Kate and Lou, one I'd snapped a few years back. I bit my lip recalling the memory of a normal day with the Shillings. How I wish I'd better appreciated those visits at the time. Are we ever grateful enough for those around us until it's too late?

Country honest, Marvin said, "Miss Kate, you sure look younger with your wig on!"

I chuckled.

I did have to pull Marvin aside shortly after he brought up politics with Miss Kate. "It is best not to talk about that subject with this resident. She's a liberal."

"Okay, gotcha."

I should have told him how dedicated Kate and Lou were to social causes, even well into their seventies. As an example, there was a factory in Brevard, whose workers went on strike. The Shillings walked the picket lines with them making sure the marchers had plenty of hot coffee and donuts.

"You two are a couple of old Trotskyites," Jamey teased.

"Thank you," they replied in tandem.

Kate and I had lunch in the dining room. Much to my relief, she didn't seem to notice most of our fellow diners were incapacitated in one way or another. After more than four decades of eating every meal with Lou, Kate amazingly didn't object to eating in a room filled with strangers. God's mercy was hard at work.

One sweet dining memory comes to mind. We'd met Kate and Lou for lunch in a restaurant near Highlands. The Shillings had driven down from Brevard and we up from Atlanta. When our foursome took our seats at a rectangular table in the rustic mountain spot, Kate looked across at Lou. She appeared agitated.

"Oh, Lou, we've never been seated this far from one another."

Without saying a word, Jamey and I got up and traded chairs so the lovebirds could sit closer together.

While visiting Kate in Monroe, I lost track of the time and arrived at Wieuca Animal Clinic shortly before the office closed. Cassie, another one of God's angels, brought the pup out to me.

"Hey, little girl. Yikes! You're bald!"

Tallee's back was completely shaved revealing splotchy pink, white, and red skin. She resembled an ottoman with a quilt folded atop. Who would possibly want the pooch now?

Cassie said, "Not to worry, Mrs. Propst, her coat will grow back in six weeks. Besides, Tallee feels so much better. Also I've weighed her and she's lost ten pounds since the last report from her vet in Athens. Tallee is now a svelte seventy-six pounds!"

I beamed. Our enforced boot camp of walking the pup and feeding her less had paid off.

"Mrs. Propst," began Cassie. "I have fallen in love with Tallee. Do you think Mrs. Shilling might consider letting me adopt her?"

I may have dropped to my knees. I may have burst into tears. I can't recall. This was a miracle of the first order.

"If it's all right, I'd like to take Tallee home tomorrow for a practice weekend with my roommates. We have two dogs and a kitty."

My enthusiasm popped like a soap bubble. Tallee had never been around other dogs. To top it off, there was a cat. God forbid.

Maybe, just maybe . . .

We'd considered trying to keep Tallee ourselves. However, after the series of pee and poo events, along with our Bella's impending nervous breakdown, we had to abandon that idea. This is said with gratitude to Jackie White, who volunteered to drive Tallee to Gainesville to a "No Kill" shelter, to Helen Reppert's son, Stephen, who offered to take Tallee into his home, and to the Millkeys, the O'Connor's, and to Janet Wells and Beverly Key, all of whom tried to find her a family. God bless these animal lovers!

"All right, Cassie, if you want to try."

"I sure do."

At noon sharp on Saturday, we delivered Tallee to the vet's office with her toys, leash, treats, and her large metal crate. Cassie greeted her warmly. She and Jamey hoisted the still portly pooch into her car.

I took Bella on a long walk promising us both better days ahead.

"Let it be."

Early that evening, Cassie sent us a text. Seeing her name, my stomach flipped. An attached photo showed Tallee sleeping happily.

"She's doing fine," typed Cassie. "We want her!"

"Kate, our vet, Dr. Smith, has a nurse named Cassie. She is a very sweet young lady who wants to take care of Tallee for us."

"I cannot take care of my Tallee, can I?"

"I don't think you can."

"Does the lady love my Tallee?"

"Very much."

"Then I believe I must love Tallee enough to let her go."

To this day, Kate's caring sacrifice for her beloved pet makes me emotional.

Cassie adopted Tallee on Monday, September 28. The dog continues to thrive. Her ears healed. Her coat returned. She enjoys her fellow pets and is a healthy sixty-five-pounder, who scurries up and down the deck steps to her yard.

There has been no further news of a butterfly delivery. Maybe that present was something Tallee reserved for the Shillings alone.

Progress at Home and in Monroe

Our postman, T.C., stopped Bella and me as we were walking a couple of blocks from home.

He whispered reverently, "I've delivered someone's cremains to your house."

"It's our friend, Lou."

"I'm sorry."

"Me, too."

"Best hurry," said T.C. "Looks like rain."

"We are on our way. Thank you, T.C."

We planned for Lou's ashes to remain with us until Kate passed away. Jamey and I would then fulfill their wishes and spread their ashes in the woods behind *The Homestead*.

I emailed a couple of close friends with a recent update.

Another of Kate's former students, our friend Kathleen, replied quickly with these words, "May the Angel of Death visit again soon."

I laughed out loud!

I giggled again as I reread her wonderfully theatrical yet sincere prayer. A caring friend, Kathleen understood the major toll the situation was taking on Jamey and me.

As a selfish, stressed-to-the-max caregiver, I hoped Kathleen's angel was warming up her wings.

Kate, comfortable in the assisted living facility. Check.

Tallee, home with Cassie. Check.

The Shillings' car sold. Check. (Bernice's father bought it.)

I spent my days with Kate at Hollander, while Jamey cleaned, met with workmen, and searched Lou's files for any overlooked monies. The widow lady was pleasant and grateful to me and to Jamey, telling me over and over to thank Jamey for his help.

"The food is good," she beamed, asking again how to find the dining room.

"Someone will come get you for your meals," I explained. "There's no need to worry."

Kate made a note. "Will come get me for supper."

"What's today?"

"Tuesday, September 28."

Another note.

"When did Lou die?"

"Two weeks ago at 5:30 p.m."

Another note.

We practiced with her television clicker. I wasn't convinced Kate would ever master the skill. Jessica, an industrious staff member, created a 1-2-3 chart for her. Hope blooms eternal. I also met Sue, the cleaning lady, who'd become my friend and a tremendous support for Kate and for me. Encouraged, I drove home to prepare dinner for my hardworking husband.

My cellphone rang as I pulled into our garage.

"Oh, how sweet," I thought. "Kate must be calling to make certain I'm home."

I'd always called the Shillings to confirm I was getting close to my house. Lou would answer on the second ring, thank me for coming, mention how much they enjoyed lunch, and say a quick goodbye. Ours was always a short conversation because Kate and Lou didn't want me to have an accident.

"Milam!" Using her authoritative voice, my teacher demanded, "You and Jamey must come get me tomorrow morning, first thing!"

I don't remember a word I said, but, Lord have mercy, was I ever crushed.

We did not go get her as she'd ordered.

Their Story

In the beginning, I was going to write about Kate and Lou, a nun who married a priest and lived happily ever after. It was to be their love story, a true to life fairytale.

Sister Thomas Margaret was the best high school English teacher. At least, she was the best teacher I experienced and remains the primary reason I developed enough confidence to write nine books, this being number ten.

My Nun and Her Husband was going to be about a smart, feisty nun and an intelligent Catholic priest. Each was as committed to the convent and to the priesthood as they would ultimately be to one another. On several occasions, Kate and Lou asked me to tell their story. However, I never quite succeeded in getting many details from them. Lou did mention he'd served for four years in the U.S. Navy before becoming a priest. Good to know!

The following is the core of what they wanted me to share with readers.

"Sister Thomas Margaret," said a breathless Sister Grace Marie, "this desk is much too heavy for us to move. Let's ask the new priest for his help."

When the handsome Father Shilling walked through the classroom door, their worlds flipped upside down and turned inside out. Kate often revisited the story of their initial meeting. With her beloved Lou nodding in agreement, she shared the life changing episode with me.

Getting lost in her husband's eyes, "It was love at first sight."

"I did move the desk!" laughed Lou.

I pushed for additional information. No deal. The two hopped up.

"That's all you need to know for now, Milam," said Kate.

"We'd better get to the restaurant before the lunch crowd arrives," warned Lou. "We don't want to have to wait for a table."

"Did you go to the seminary immediately after your stint in the Navy?"

"Kate, did Milam ask me a question?"

"I don't think so, Lou."

"Okay, you two. I get it. Are we going to Wendy's or to Barberito's?"

Our Reconnection

My first book, *A Flower Blooms on Charlotte Street*, had been published by Mercer University Press. Naturally, I was very excited to share the novel with my English teacher. I drove over to St. Pius, book in hand, to try to track down the whereabouts of Sister Thomas Margaret. I'd mentioned her name in the book's acknowledgements.

I was greeted with the somber news she was gone.

"Dead!"

"Oh no, she's left the convent."

I was relieved and I was curious.

I've already chronicled this in another book, *Writer, Writer*. In a nutshell, my friend Georganne knew Sister Mary Susan, who was Sister Thomas Margaret's best buddy at St. Pius. In turn, Sister Mary Susan contacted a priest, Father Harrison, who had a current address for her. I was thrilled to discover the now married nun (oh my!) lived near Asheville, North Carolina, which, coincidentally, is the setting for *Charlotte Street*.

I immediately mailed her a signed copy with a thank you message. Much to my surprise and delight, she responded, "Old English teachers often haunt their students. In this case, the student has come back to haunt the old English teacher."

She included an eighteen-page critique with one suggestion. My teacher wanted me to write a sequel (which I did, four of them, in fact). Best of all, she liked my work. Her exact words were, "It's the closest thing to *To Kill a Mockingbird* any student of mine has written."

Obviously, *Charlotte Street* is a far cry from Harper Lee's remarkable book. Nonetheless, I was flattered beyond measure.

An aside: Kate so loved *To Kill a Mockingbird*, Lou nicknamed her "Scout" in honor of the protagonist.

Since our reconnection in 1999, Jamey and I have occupied a small niche in the Shillings' comfortable world. We've shared many conversations and many meals. That said, it seems the more we've learned about the couple, the more mystery surrounds them. What I can tell the reader, for certain, is Kate and Lou have never once had an argument. I've questioned them about their claim many a time. Their answer was always the same.

"We don't argue about anything," Lou insisted.

"Now we might discuss something," explained Kate. "but there's never a cross word between us. Never."

"Never," echoed Lou.

I've known very few couples as congenial and content. Could Kate and Lou's successful marriage be the result of years of serving others as a nun and a priest? Whenever I shared that concept with them, they both laughed heartedly.

Laugh though they did, I believe I'm right.

The Habit of Sister Thomas Margaret

I have two more stories to share about Kate, the Catholic nun. Each has to do with her religious habit, or as she termed it, "the outfit."

Kate frequently cared for her aging parents and often spent holidays with them. Of course, the Small's dutiful daughter was always dressed head to toe in the long black habit and veil of her religious order.

"I was staying with Mom and Pop on Halloween. Naturally, I insisted on passing out the goodies to neighborhood Trick or Treaters."

As she told the story, she turned to Lou, who grinned and nodded.

"More and more children appeared," she continued. "I started noticing that the same little spooks returned over and over again."

"Now, boys and girls, that's quite enough," she admonished sternly. "You must leave some candy for the others."

"See!" said one particularly disgruntled little fellow. "I told you there was a really, truly witch at this house!"

"Great story, Scout," said Lou. "I never tire of your telling it."

The second incident occurred after Kate made her decision to leave the convent. Still dressed as a Sister of St. Joseph, she drove over to the University of Georgia to apply for a job in the English department.

"They hired me on the spot!" she boasted.

"Miss Small, I'm offering this position contingent on one stipulation," said the professor. He pointed to her habit. "You cannot wear that to teach at UGA."

"Why would I?"

She rose from her seat and walked toward the door. Looking back over her shoulder, Kate announced, "I can start whenever you like."

Her job secured, Kate turned in her habit and went shopping for civilian clothes.

Not long after, she returned to Athens with a second mission. That time her recently *widowed mother went along.

*Sadly, Pop passed away in 1965 and didn't live long enough to see his cherished daughter happily married.

"Pull in over there, Kate," said Mrs. Small pointing to a parking place. "That gentleman appears to have some authority."

"How do you know?"

"He's smoking a pipe. Honk your horn, Kate."

Honk, honk.

"May I help you ladies?" responded the somewhat apprehensive professor.

Kate wanted to gather information for Lou. "Our friend is retired military," she explained. "He hopes to pursue a graduate degree in psychology."

As if the Heavens parted to announce God's long range plans for the Shillings, the random man turned out to be the very professor, who advised Lou all throughout his studies for his doctorate.

It is important to note, the nun and the priest went through the proper channels of the Catholic Church to be released from their religious vows.

Sister Grace Marie, Kate's Superior and dear friend, commented, "You two did everything the right way. Now go with God's blessings and with mine as you both follow your hearts."

Entering graduate school, Lou took a room in an Athens boarding house. Kate and her mother lived in a small rental home, which was convenient to the university campus, where she taught English.

After Mrs. Small's death, the Shillings were quietly married.

Ups and Downs and Ups in Apartment 17

We'd started off pretty well at Hollander. Kate was surrounded by the familiar items of her life including books, music, and the Shillings' paintings and photographs. Several pictures of Tallee were prominently displayed. Her photo with Lou, one I'd taken in front of *The Homestead*, was in clear view. I moved her two favorite pictures of her husband to the bedside table.

The optimist in me assumed we'd continue to make progress. Wrong! I was talking almost daily with her patient nurses.

"It's normal for our new residents to become agitated."

"There's always a period of adjustment."

"Of course, Miss Kate is confused."

"Hopefully, she won't plead with you to take her home next time you visit."

"We're encouraging her to spend more time in the lobby. People are coming and going all day keeping our residents occupied."

"Maybe Miss Kate will agree to participate in our group activities."

A physician's assistant was coming Tuesday to evaluate Kate for anti-depressants. That would be a big change for a woman who never took as much as an aspirin.

More prayers; for what, I knew not. The situation was becoming an emotional and financial burden for which Jamey and I were ill prepared. It was a different experience from caring for our own elderly family members. As Jamey and I tried to navigate the sea of problems, with its occasional rogue wave, I stopped pleading with Kathleen's Angel of Death to appear. It was obvious the angel was not paying me the least bit of attention.

Perhaps the Angel of Death was saying, "Not just yet. Be patient."

I was putting laundry in the dryer. Jamey was nearby in his office, attempting to close out one of Lou's numerous small online bank accounts. Even with all the Shillings' identifications in his hands, the bank required an answer to a security question.

*When caregivers are not "blood kin," red tape can strangle an honest person who's simply trying to help. Jamey's hours on the phone were driving my husband out of his mind.

He exploded, "How the hell do I know the name of Lou's favorite singer?"

From the laundry room, I shouted, "Renee Fleming!"

The woman on the other end of the speaker phone exclaimed, "That's right!"

"I'll be damned," said Jamey.

We celebrated at Subway with a tuna sandwich.

Not long after the Renee Fleming triumph, Kate and I experienced one of our better visits. Her caregivers told me I am often credited by Kate with decorating her pretty apartment. Hoorah for me, I'd managed to please "STM."

Back in the fifties, the nun used two ink stamps to grade our less than perfect efforts. One read, (same old) "76," which encouraged the student to stretch himself or herself a little bit more. The other, far more critical, were the initials for Sister Thomas Margaret, "STM." She'd stamp an entire first page of a paper with those damning letters meaning "absolutely dreadful, now start over again."

I like to believe I never received either condemnation. Still the "76" resides somewhere deep down in my long erased memory. Throughout the years, as I write books, I fear penning the same old seventy-six.

Something Kate consistently praised about Hollander was the food, which was a great improvement over Lou's cuisine.

To defend her husband's cooking, Lou did get off to a rather late start with his culinary skills. First a son, then a college student, then a Navy man, and onto the priesthood prior to his marriage; Lou had never, ever cooked. Age eighty is not the optimum time to learn how to prepare three daily meals.

Cooking aside, I commend Kate's late husband for his unlimited devotion to his wife. Only once I inquired as to how he was doing.

Lou replied, "I am doing fine."

"Lou," I argued, "Kate's dementia must be awfully hard on you."

"No, Milam!" he frowned. "It is an honor to care for Scout. She's my world."

The Shillings' marriage was far from the same old seventy-six.

Random Notes from the First Months

Kate and I were relaxing on the porch which overlooks a pond. We saw two white ducks and I admired the knockout rose bushes.

"Kate, look at the roses. They remind me of the ones Lou planted by your patio."

She made no comment.

I yearned for one more morning, a morning when everything was fine with the Shillings and Tallee. I wanted to enjoy the three of them, worry-free.

Antonio, a kitchen worker, came outside.

"Sometimes, when you're not here, I bring Miss Kate out to the porch."

"Thank you, Antonio."

Kate, emotionless, stared at the roses. What, if anything, was she remembering?

At 3:30, Tia came to Kate's room bringing lemonade, a Hollander tradition. As she served the cold drink, Tia asked my permission to introduce her husband to Kate. A former English teacher, Charles had to retire early due to serious heart surgery.

"You'd enjoy talking with another teacher, wouldn't you, Kate?"

She sipped her lemonade and nodded her approval.

"Miss Kate, if it's all right with you, Charles and I will come by tomorrow afternoon."

"Remember to bring an extra lemonade for him."

Kate always liked to provide treats for others. Every time I left the Shillings' home, she sent me off with a goodie bag with bottled water, a diet drink, cookies, and chocolate. It was our tradition.

"Kate, what do you think about sharing one of your books with Tia and her husband?"

"Yes. Give her *Emily's Laughter*."

"Thank you, Miss Kate. Charles and I will enjoy reading your book."

"You're welcome," said Kate. "Now take good care of Emily. A great deal of work went into her."

"I promise you Emily Dickinson will be in very good hands." Tia gave Kate a hug. "We'll see you tomorrow."

I reflected on Kate's having dedicated her entire life to writing, which included her beautiful poetry. I walked to the wall by her French doors and admired the treasured award from the Amherst Society.

Certificate of Achievement in Poetry is hereby awarded by the Amherst Society to Catherine S. Shilling to recognize acceptance for inclusion in the American Poetry Annual. Presented to commend artistry in poetry on April 5th 1998 by Paul L. Brodes, Executive Director the Amherst Society.

In addition to her two Masters and Lou's Ph.D., this was the only certificate the Shillings chose to display. Kate and Lou tended to downplay their numerous accomplishments.

Ours had been a very nice day, one I almost ruined by getting lost trying to find a shortcut home. My mistake doubled the already one hour's drive. Emily Dickinson was surely laughing. *Emily* was *laughing* at me.

Years ago, when I was trying to master the less traveled road to the Shillings' house, I took a wrong turn. I called them to explain the problem. Kate and Lou were very punctual people and expected me to be the same way.

Lou answered the phone. "Is something wrong? Where are you?"

"Lost!"

"Are there any road signs?"

I told him I was somewhere on Athens Highway 10.

"Not too bad," said Lou. "Tell me what you see."

"A large shopping mall." I mentioned names of a couple of stores.

"Good. I got you. Now get into the right lane . . . "

A fine teacher in his own right, the man knew how to guide me to the safety of *The Homestead*. Lou kept me on the phone for the remainder of my drive. I can still see him standing on his driveway waving wildly as he tried hard not to make fun of me. Kate was waiting in their car. I parked out front and off we went to Jason's Deli.

Blessed Support

Arriving at home, I sent out an email update about Kate to several friends and Pius alums. Everyone wrote back with messages of concern. Sandy, BA, and Trudy asked for Kate's address to send her cards. Others offered encouragement. Many said they were praying.

One response came from Bev Gibbs Riccardi, who extended kind words of praise not only for Kate, but also for us. I quickly answered, *"Any stars in our crowns are long gone, Bev, due to Jamey's grumbling and my making jokes and/or complaining."*

She responded. I include Bev's email because her words uplifted me for a solid week.

"Sister Thomas Margaret may not know, at every moment, what you both have done for her, but she will remember, in fragments, how lucky she is to have friends like you and Jamey."

Thank you, Bev.

I was off to purchase two pairs of size 3X petite pajamas. I laughed as I wrote on my list, "petite." Another star from my crown crashed to the floor.

I finally got in touch with Lou's one friend, Ed, who was a fellow the Shillings occasionally met at the Starbucks in Barnes & Noble. I'd called the cafe asking the manager to display a note with my cellphone number: "To Ed, friend of an elderly intellectual couple. Clue, the lady arrives in a wheelchair."

I hit pay dirt. Ed called.

He was shocked to learn of Lou's sudden death. Like us, like Trudy, he assumed Lou would outlive Kate.

"Thanks for your note," he began. "I was worried when the Shillings didn't show up for such a long time. I even searched the obituaries for one of their names."

The nice man visited Kate a few times.

It never occurred to me to put anything in the paper about Lou's passing. If I had, I know Lou Shilling wouldn't have approved. A long time ago, during one of our patio conversations, he pointed to the woods and made the following statement.

"Scout and I want our ashes to be dispersed out there in our woods. No obituary, no ceremony, no big to do."

He took Kate's hand. They nodded in agreement.

"Milam, don't beat yourself up for not writing Lou's obit," comforted Jamey. "Ed would have been the only reader who knew him."

"Such a sad commentary."

"Hey, Baby Doll, they were happy."

"You're right. That they were."

Bernice had not finished at the house as she'd promised, so my industrious husband took charge. He rented a truck and hired a man to help carry things to the local dump. And, because we had been unable to find a handyman, Jamey repaired the damage under the kitchen sink. Thank goodness my father-in-law, Ed Propst, taught his son how to fix things.

We'd never paid any attention to the house's problems. Why should we? The home wasn't ours.

We also weren't concerned anytime Lou and Kate joked about their money matters.

"Kate and I are going to win the lottery!"

We'd all have a big laugh.

The trouble was Lou was not joking. The Publisher's Clearing House Sweepstakes was a significant component of his long term financial plan.

The Bank

October 16, one month and two days after Lou's death, we went to the bank requesting the Shillings' house payment be forgiven until after their home was sold. No deal. As Jamey pointed out, it was worth a shot.

"Sam," I interjected, "Should we reconsider selling the house 'as is'?"

A good man, he listened patiently.

"The entire inside needs a fresh coat of paint," I began. "There's considerable water damage from a leaky roof, and the vacuum cleaner burned up from Jamey's trying to rid the carpet of dog hair."

The banker rolled his eyes.

"For us to take proper care of Mrs. Shilling," added Jamey, "we must get as much money out of her house as we can."

"I understand," replied Sam. He scratched his chin and pulled up some numbers. "I think you should make the repairs."

"Done!"

Jamey immediately contacted Teresa, our real estate agent, to tell her about the new plan. I called Travis (A+ Painters), the husband of LaShayla (Advance Care), who agreed to paint the inside, AND he had a carpet guy! As soon as Travis and his rug buddy could finish, we'd put the house on the market for $120,000.

Bernice resurfaced!!! Seems she'd been sick with gout. On top of that, her cellphone with our number, had been lost for days. I simply must share the following story.

"Bernice," said her grandmother, "my purse is singing!"

"Singing to you is it?"

"Don't make fun of me. Listen."

Bernice heard nothing and thought to herself how sad dementia can be.

"I am telling you, child, it sings to me!"

Bernice giggled a bit and excused herself to the kitchen to prepare the two a cup of tea.

Suddenly her grandmother shouted from her bedroom, "Come in here, child, and listen for yourself!"

Bernice recognized a familiar ring tone. She reached into

her grandmother's singing purse and retrieved her phone.

Her first text was to me. "I can finish the cleanup at the house now."

I wrote back, "Thanks much, Bernice, but we're all done."

Angel reinstated.

We sent in the required forms to the Veterans Administration in hopes of getting a few dollars in widow's benefits from Lou's four years in the Navy. When I told Kate the news about her home's being redone and about the VA, she acted pleased.

She immediately asked if we'd sold the house. "Not yet, Jamey has a lot of work to do."

"Oh, I see."

Looking her straight in the eye, I said, "Please trust us."

"I do."

I squeezed her hand and wondered to myself if I actually trusted us. How could we continue to pay all the bills? The Shillings' money was pouring out like sand through a sieve.

"Has the house sold?" she asked again.

"No, Kate, not yet."

"Is Tallee with you?"

"Kate, Tallee is with our veterinarian's nurse, Cassie."

"Does she love my Tallee?"

"Very much. Tallee now has three people, including Nurse Cassie, and two dogs, and a cat to keep her entertained." I added, "Tallee has lost twenty pounds running around in Cassie's backyard."

"When I get stronger," said Kate, "we'll bring Tallee here."

"Okay," I lied.

"Have we sold the house?"

"Not yet."

I was baffled yet relieved that Kate wasn't mourning the loss of her home. Indeed, she wanted it to be sold. Had she completely forgotten about a place, which filled her with so much pride?

When I showed Kate the picture of herself, Lou, and

Tallee out front, a shot taken only three years prior, she made no comment whatsoever. It was as if Kate were looking at a magazine advertisement with total strangers standing by the front entrance to someone else's house.

The Gift

"Look at the little dog," Kate exclaimed "Isn't he cute!"

We paused to admire a ceramic yellow lab outside the door of another Hollander resident. As we continued to our noontime meal, I wished to myself I could find a similar one for Kate. She'd have her own Tallee, yes, but a Tallee, who'd not have to be fed or walked or cared for in anyway.

Jamey frequents Goodwill stores on Tuesdays, the day senior citizens receive a twenty percent discount. His hobby keeps him occupied. My husband purchases items to sell on Ebay. He uses his fun money to spend on our grandsons. Occasionally I'll go along with him to see what treasures I might find.

We drove to a Goodwill north of Atlanta. As Jamey headed toward men's shirts, I went to the back of the store looking for the ladies' room. Out of the corner of my eye, I spotted IT! There on the shelf, surrounded by figurines and holiday items, sat a statue of a yellow lab, very similar to the one Kate had admired. I couldn't believe my good fortune. I tucked it under my arm and made a beeline for Jamey.

Holding the item aloft like a Super Bowl trophy, I shouted, "I found a Tallee!"

"Kate doesn't want that thing," he grimaced. "Look, Milam, it has a big crack."

I would not be denied.

"You can fix it. You can fix anything."

I pointed out the damage was located exactly where Tallee's hot spots had been.

"Lest you forget, Jamey Propst, the hot spots lead us to Cassie."

I watched Jamey as he repaired the ceramic pooch. I had to laugh. He may never be free of his Damn Dog.

Kate had a fit over her new Tallee. She absolutely loved her! We placed the statue in several spots around the apartment.

"Not on the floor," she warned. "Someone might kick her over."

"How about in your bedroom?"

"No, I only sleep in there. I want to be able to look at Tallee all day long."

We finally settled on putting her by the television.

"She's so beautiful."

Kate often used those same words when she petted the real Tallee. Were my tears for joy or for sorrow? I couldn't say which.

As guilty as we felt giving Tallee to Cassie, we realized it was the best thing for the dog. I let Kate continue to believe she might again care for her pet. Shame on me for lying to anyone, especially for lying to my nun.

Kate asked me to show her where I'd displayed a recent photo of Jamey and me.

"I can't see it clearly. Next time you come, I want you to bring me a large copy, an 8X10."

Yes, Sister."

Our Routine

As I write this story, I'm pleased I kept notes. I'm not creative enough to make up this stuff.

Sheila stuck her head in the door and asked if she might introduce us to a prospective resident.

"Miss Kate, may I show off your apartment?"

"Please come in," said Kate.

As we stood aside, Sheila, along with an older lady and her daughter admired the Shillings' artwork. I was grateful we'd finally gotten everything arranged to my nun's liking. Unusually animated on that particular day, Kate went on about how much she enjoyed being at Hollander.

"It's very pretty here and the food is great." She added, "The people are all quite nice."

Sheila glowed.

After I added my two cents worth, the lady's daughter said, "Sheila, you should hire these two to do promotions."

I never thought Kate could be as content, especially given her first few weeks at the facility. Earlier that morning she'd talked about the importance of keeping a positive attitude.

"It's much easier to be pleasant than it is to be mean."

During lunch she again told her tablemates, Barbara and Shirley, what a badly behaved teenager I had been. The dialogue was turning into our regular act.

"Kate, you know very well, I was as quiet as a mouse in your classroom. I was too intimidated by you not to be!"

She ignored me.

"Milam," I'd warn, "if you cannot behave, you'll have to stand out in the hall."

"You are so wrong, Kate. It was Rita Ann and Janet, who did all the talking."

Only once, she looked at me and acknowledged what I'd always known to be the truth. "You know, Milam, that does sound more like it."

"Thank you, Kate!"

The very next week, she began, "Milam," I'd say, "if you cannot behave . . ."

After dessert, our favorite part of any meal, we returned to her apartment. To my utter surprise, she commented, "I can feel Lou's presence around me. In the night, I'll reach over to his pillow only to find it empty. But I try my best not to dwell on his absence. I choose to believe he is here with me."

Ours had been a lovely visit. Perhaps Lou really was watching over our Kate, his beloved Scout.

God's Wink

Having successfully secured her father's VA benefits, my author friend, Jackie White, shared tips with me about how best to deal with bureaucrats.

"It's always best to go to the VA in person and be sure to get the names of the people in charge." she advised. "Never let up."

After my weekly visit, I stopped at a Shell service station to buy a diet Dr. Pepper and some crackers. As I am prone to do with total strangers, I told the clerk about Kate's dire financial situation.

I was about to experience a *God's Wink*. This occurs when Our Lord gives us a little wink, via an anonymous coincidence, to assure us He is working in our lives.

Handing me my change, she said, "I understand. I used to work at Hollander."

"You did?"

"Yep, it's a wonderful place."

God had just winked at me.

She proceeded to tell me about another elderly lady, one who was having to leave because her money was running out. My stomach dropped. Was this Christmas future for Kate?

"Her whole family stormed the VA."

"And?"

"The lady was able to stay."

The clerk winked, too.

Thanks to Jackie and the Shell lady, my resolve steadied. We'd take on the VA as soon as possible.

The following Saturday, we suffered a setback; make that two setbacks in less than ten minutes.

Domingo called. "The carpet, Mr. Jamey, it did not come yesterday as you said it would."

"Thanks, Domingo. I'll check into it."

Given the fact we had to have new carpet to market the house, I was surprised by Jamey's calm reply. His cellphone rang again. I assumed Domingo had something else awful to tell us. It was worse.

"The toilet is broken!" squealed the hysterical young lady, who rents our house in DeKalb County.

Still behaving in an oddly stoic manner, Jamey gathered his plumbing tools and we drove to the rental house. I continue to appreciate Jamey's father for sharing his home repair skills with my husband. Mercifully the job was a quick fix. We headed to Athens to see what the heck happened to the carpet guy.

"Let's go by Kate's on our way," I suggested. "She misses you."

Jamey replied with an unenthusiastic, "Why not."

Kate was thrilled to see Jamey.

"I believe you like Jamey more than me."

She giggled.

"When you were our teacher, you always favored the boys over the girls."

This she did not, could not deny. Sister Thomas Margaret adored the young men.

She shrugged her shoulders. I knew she knew I knew.

I noticed Jamey was digging in his pockets. He quickly excused himself and went out to our car. Returning shortly, my husband motioned for me to step into the hall.

"I forgot the damn keys!"

"What keys?"

"Kate's house keys!"

He cracked. What followed was a barrage of salty language about our rental house, the toilet, and the irresponsible carpet people. "Irresponsible" was not the word he used. None of his dialogue will I include in this chapter.

"Might Travis have the extra set?" I offered.

"Maybe. I'll try to reach him," he groused, "but he's probably busy today."

Another wink, God's plans were in place. Travis not only had the keys, but he could also could meet us at the house right away.

Explaining to Kate we had just received some good news, we said goodbye.

A bonus, Travis found another man to install the carpet and he'd set it up for us immediately. As we were chatting,

Domingo dropped by. Grinning from ear to ear, he announced, "I have a man who wants the Shillings' house!"

I couldn't believe how quickly our luck was changing. But wait a second . . .

The buyer, Domingo's best friend, was offering $50,000 less than we were asking.

Undaunted, Domingo inquired about Lou's car.

"I'm sorry," said Jamey, "but it's sold."

Twice disappointed, Domingo hung his head.

I wanted to help out the sweet-spirited neighbor. I mentioned that our son might have a car for him. I called Jay and Domingo perked up. Jay answered on the third ring. Once again the stars were aligning. I handed the phone to the excited Domingo.

Suddenly his body wobbled. "Straight shift? Oh no, sir. Oh no," he gulped. "You see, sir, I cannot drive a straight shift."

Domingo shrugged his shoulders. "That's how it goes."

To this day, I still feel disappointed for Domingo. Such a deserving man is he. From him, I was learning to take things as they come. Like the gentle neighbor, what other choice had I?

Testimonial

Encouraged by our enthusiasm for Hollander, Sheila asked if I might be willing to write something about the facility for her use. Here it is:

The day I met Sheila McArdle at Hollander Senior Living, our friend Kate Shilling's life took a turn for the better. Having lost her husband, Lou, Kate was not only facing his untimely death, but also the loss of her home and of a precious pup named Tallee.

Enter Sheila. She offered Kate a lovely new home, where our friend felt welcomed and was made comfortable as she discovered friendships among the other residents and with the caring staff. Every day Kate participates in activities including morning donuts and coffee, bingo games, and afternoon lemonade visits.

Hollander is special because it offers seniors a new lease on life. Like Kate Shilling, my husband and I are most thankful for this wonderful place.

Sincerely, Milam and Jamey Propst

People assume, because I am an author, my writing must come easily. This is not always the case. If I don't feel an honest connection with a topic, coming up with the right words presents a challenge. I was being sincere, therefore, composing the testimonial was a piece of cake for me. I hope it will help other families and friends struggling with similar situations.

Kate asked, "Did you think I could ever survive without my Lou?"

"No, Kate. I did not," I replied shaking my head in disbelief. I took her hand, "I'm extremely proud of you and astonished by resilience."

As with the testimonial, I was being totally sincere. I couldn't believe the strength of this woman. Just like in our long ago past, she was educating me, but this time, she was educating me through her example. Kate became a model of how to accept change and move forward even under unimaginably difficult circumstances. I pray I'll always remember the lessons she taught.

We ended our conversation when Sheila knocked on the door. She entered offering a tiny kitten for Kate to hold.

"Aren't you a cutie," said Kate as she caressed the adorable kitty.

"We found her out by the pond. Would you like to keep her?" asked Sheila.

I nearly fainted. The pungent scent of a dirty litter pan makes my eyes water.

As is typical for me, I rocketed from A to Z. The litter pan aside, the companionship of the kitten might relieve some of Kate's overwhelming loneliness. She was always begging the staff to sit with her.

When I visited her, should I as much as open my purse, she'd start to fret.

"You aren't looking for your car keys, are you?"

Kate would plead with me to stay a little while longer.

"A few more minutes," she'd begin as she reached for her tablet. "I must have something else to discuss with you."

Maybe a pet, one not requiring walks, might be a good idea. Surely someone could clean the litter pan.

"No thank you," said Kate. "I really don't like cats."

She handed the kitten to Sheila.

"I totally understand." Sheila and the baby kitten left to visit another resident.

We'd dodged a bullet.

"Luckily, it wasn't a puppy," said Kate. "I would have kept a dog!"

Downward Spiral

Kate became more and more confused throughout December. A noticeable change came only two weeks after Linda Kelleher's visit. When Jamey and I arrived for the Hollander Christmas party, we detected a big difference in her demeanor.

"Ready to go to the party?"

"Party?"

Unenthused and distant, she wasn't the least bit excited to see us. I glanced at Linda's tree and wished Kate were Kate.

The staff, beautifully dressed in holiday attire, had gone all out for the residents and their families with scrumptious food, desserts galore, holiday music, and Santa Claus, to boot. Within an hour, Kate didn't remember we'd been to a party, not even when I showed her the fun photo of herself taken with Santa.

The following is an email I sent to Trudy on January 18, 2016.

Dear Trudy,

It's Monday morning; I've tossed and turned all night long. As I wrote to you yesterday, Kate's mind has gone to mush. I went again to Athens Regional Hospital yesterday to find her more confused than ever. She had no memory of our being there all day Saturday. The single thing she talked about was finding her shoes. They're keeping her in bed because she's even more prone to falling. She is eating and drinking but makes little sense. Agitated and anxious, Kate thrashed about in the bed, again wanting her shoes.

The doctor came and asked a battery of questions. All I could say was she's gone downhill drastically in the last four weeks. The tests showed no stroke, only the previously mentioned heart issues, which we've known about. She's now being treated with pills, no more drips.

Kate did know me Saturday and Sunday, an improvement, because she had not known either Jamey or me at Hollander on the previous Saturday (January 9). Her recent fall precipitated the ambulance ride to Athens Regional.

Jamey and I went to check out Northeast Rehab here in Atlanta, near us and St. Joseph's Hospital. Father Steve, our trusted priest and the hospital chaplain, recommends the place. Plus, my friend BA's Uncle John was there for months. There is an available room, semiprivate. They take Medicare and then Medicaid once Kate's funds run out. I hate to think of her being in a shared room, but we may no choice. Barring a miracle, she will require care twenty-four, seven.

No nibbles on the house as yet.

That's the situation, Trudy. I'll know more later today and will email you. I've prayed for Lou to come get his Kate. Wish he would! Like everything else, this, too, will pass. The Good Lord is in charge.

Love, Milam

There's one thing I didn't mention in Trudy's email. Melissa, the social worker we met the very first day at Athens Regional, greeted us on Saturday in the emergency room. It was encouraging to see Melissa again, the first angel who came to our aid. Her kindness reminded me God remains near.

"Lou, please come for your beloved Kate before we have to put her in Northeast. Lord, hear my prayer."

He heard me!!!!

The last day of Kate's third and longest stay at Athens Regional Hospital, her most unsettling, two of Hollander's finest professionals called. Both encouraged us to let them continue to care for "our Miss Kate."

One was Susan, Kate's attentive and caring nurse. Without Susan, I'd have fallen to pieces on any number of occasions. Not only could Susan explain medical problems in layman's terms, but she always offered words of encouragement and hope.

The second call came from Oree, the *new manager of Hollander.

*I had been near hysterics when Sheila moved up to corporate. For me it was the straw that broke the camel's back (I being the camel). However, my initial meeting with Oree assured me Kate remained in excellent hands. He is a hugger, a man who loves his residents. Oree also understands how to reassure their families. He urged us to bring Miss Kate "home" to Hollander.

"I didn't think you would be able take care of Kate in her present condition?"

"Why not? Everyone here adores her. Will you please trust us with Miss Kate?"

When I mentioned our money worries, the gentle man replied, "I have your back."

A devout Catholic, Oree would spend a few minutes to pray the rosary with the former nun. He's a dear.

I put aside the paperwork for Northeast.

Connections

Things improved for Kate following her extremely unsettling hospital stay. Thanks to Susan's phone call and Oree's encouragement, Kate returned to Hollander. Once her medications were stabilized, she again became *almost* herself. Our routine returned to its *new* normal.

This chapter is about a quite curious coincidence, one which weaves together Kate, another Hollander resident, Linda (St. Pius alum), and a WWII tragedy.

"My Christmas tree is so nice," Kate often said.

I'd show her the photo taken with Linda.

"Oh yes, the Euart girl."

The Euart girl is a person who delights in making what she terms, "connections." This chapter is dedicated to her.

Walking toward Apartment 17, I was stopped by Lanie, Kate's Occupational Therapist. I assumed she wanted to update me on my nun.

"Do you want to meet someone very special?" she began. "He's a WWII veteran."

"Of course, I do."

Lanie turned her palm toward a charming gentleman, who was pushing his wife in a wheelchair, "This is Hollis Johnson and his wife, Dolly."

"I'm honored to meet you both. Thank you, Mr. Johnson, for your service to our country."

"Thank you, ma'am."

When Hollis tipped his hat, I noticed a symbol for WWII, the Southwest Pacific theater.

I couldn't help myself, I blurted out the name of Linda's uncle, Captain Elwood Joseph Euart. Only the week before, Linda had shared his story with me. She told me how her father's brother rescued many of his fellow soldiers as his troopship tipped over after hitting two mines. Some seventy-four years later, divers discovered Euart's remains.

"Was it the SS President Coolidge?"

"Yes, Hollis, it was. How in the world could you possibly know?"

"I was there."

"You were there?"

"Yes, I watched the Coolidge sink," he stated sadly. "My ship, the USS Chester, was anchored in the harbor."

"According to the scuttlebutt," added Hollis, "your friend's uncle was quite a hero."

I couldn't believe my ears. I called Linda on my way home.

"May I ride to Hollander with you next time you go?" she asked. "I'd love to meet this gentleman!"

Their meeting was extraordinary. Linda showed Hollis the scrapbook she'd compiled filled with information and pictures of her family's hero, Capt. Elwood Euart. Hollis was "introduced" to the man he had only heard about, a man everyone in the harbor (Espiritu Santo in the New Hebrides) knew as the incredibly brave soldier who sacrificed his all for others.

Hollis showed Linda a picture of his own ship. His hand firm, he put the point of his ballpoint pen on the front of the deck.

"This is exactly where I was standing when your uncle's ship went down."

We sat transfixed.

"Hollis, you are the only person I've ever met, who witnessed Uncle Elwood's death."

We all had tears.

Linda told Hollis and Dolly her uncle had been an excellent swimmer; that his family couldn't fathom how he could have drowned. At least, they didn't understand until the whole story came out. Elwood had made it to safety, but he was told several men were still trapped down in the infirmary. He tied a rope around himself and rescued more than a half dozen men. With everyone safely out, everyone but Capt. Euart, the SS Coolidge slid off the reef, and the brave captain was lost. He was posthumously awarded the Distinguished Service Cross.

The story doesn't end there. A couple of years ago, divers discovered the remains of Capt. Euart, along with his military dog tags, and other material evidence. DNA testing was done to establish his identity. In August of 2016, the soldier's remains were returned to Rhode Island, where he was buried with his family and with his father Elwood, who never gave up hope his son's remains would eventually come home. The church was full for the funeral Mass, full of family and family friends, full of military representatives, of state and local dignitaries, and full of

Boy Scouts, who represented Elwood's troop. At last count, five Euarts have carried the name of Elwood. Rightfully so.

I was pleased Linda could make the connection with Hollis Johnson. What a remarkable twist of fate it was that our high school teacher just happened to live in Monroe, Georgia, only a few short steps down the hall from the Johnsons.

Ash Wednesday

Before Lou was taken off life support, Jamey whispered to me, "We've got to make sure Lou has the Last Rites."

"I never thought about that."

I don't know how Jamey pulled off this feat, but all of a sudden there stood a priest, praying over Lou and administering the Last Rites of the Catholic Church. At very least, the brief service gave my husband the assurance he'd done everything he could for the former priest.

Trudy and I will forever appreciate his thoughtfulness. In thanking him, Lou's sister commented, "Our mother would be most grateful to Jamey."

During the winter of 2016, as Kate came and went physically and mentally, Jamey continued to obsess over the state of her soul. He shouldn't have worried because God had already set in place what was to happen.

On Ash Wednesday, as we were leaving Hollander much later than usual, my husband noticed a man coming toward us from the parking lot.

"Excuse me, sir. Are you a priest, a Catholic priest?"

"Yes, I am."

The next thing I knew, Kate, Jamey, and I were grouped with several other residents around an improvised altar in Hollander's activity room. The scene was reminiscent of The Last Supper as we encircled the priest while he conducted an Ash Wednesday service. It culminated with Kate's receiving the Sacrament of the Sick.

Jamey assisted the former nun in making the Sign of the Cross.

"Please, Kate, give me your hand," he began. Jamey tenderly guided her fingers to her forehead. "In the name of the Father, and of the Son, and of the Holy Spirit."

The group responded, "Amen."

This was a blessed moment for all of us in that holy room. Kate may not have understood exactly what was going on, but she was smiling peacefully. Lou had to have been somewhere nearby.

Was the prior Father Shilling aware of his own last sacrament a few months before? We wanted to believe he was.

To us, both blessed sacraments felt very meaningful and certainly filled with grace.

Stars adorn my husband's crown.

Beach Volleyball

Some three or four contracts had fallen through on the Shillings' house. We'd lost count. Jamey and I were getting more and more anxious but remained determined to keep Kate at Hollander. Additionally, we had a growing stack of unpaid bills for her. I continued to assure Kate she had nothing about which to be concerned.

"You have plenty of money," I lied. "Not to worry."

Did she know? I think not.

"Just keep taking your medicine," I advised, "so your brain can remain clear."

"I will."

"I'm proud of you, Kate, and of your determination to keep going with physical therapy."

I joined her for the morning's exercise class. Nine of us sat in a circle of chairs doing a variety of calisthenics. Seated, we raised our arms, reached and stretched, and we lifted our legs. After warming up, we played games, one involved a beach ball.

Marie, the activities director, shouted enthusiastically, "Class, are you ready?"

"READY!!!"

The beach ball shot toward me. I ducked. What a humiliating moment! Retrieving the ball, I gingerly lobbed it toward a pretty lady across the circle from us. She fired it back at me. Our fellow players were obviously taking the game more seriously than I'd anticipated. When the ball came toward Kate, she knocked the stew out of it!

"You go, girl," I cheered.

I assumed Kate's invigorated hit was a fluke. Wrong! She blasted that ball again and again and AGAIN. At one point, my nun reached across my chest to protect me from getting struck!

"Miss Kate is our best beach volleyball player," announced Marie.

Who knew the nun was so competitive?

Our friend Nedom knew. Kate was once his baseball umpire!

Nedom Haley and his wife, Carol, go to our church. He frequently asks how my nun, our nun, is getting along. Kate had taught him, too. How many students had the exceptional teacher impacted throughout her twenty-two plus years as a Sister of St. Joseph?

Nedom previously mentioned he was in her class at the old Sacred Heart School in downtown Atlanta.

"I was her top student," he boasted.

Easy to believe; Nedom, an attorney, is a very smart man.

"You said she was your baseball umpire?"

"Sister was our umpire and our pitcher."

"She pitched, too?"

I was flabbergasted. The image of the portly nun, covered from head to toe in black, winding up for a pitch, still makes me giggle.

"She was really good," he added.

"During recess Sister Thomas Margaret was in charge of our pickup baseball games," he grinned. "Sister kept careful notes on the score, who was next up to bat, and who remained on base. The bell rang signaling the end of recess, but it was no problem for us. The next day Sister started us off exactly where we'd stopped."

Teacher, wife, mother, dog lover, writer, poet, painter, social activist, music enthusiast, football fan, friend of Flannery O'Connor, and now I learn Kate's a jock. What else am I going to discover about this woman?

At Last, a Buyer

By late spring, our real estate agent finally found a buyer for the Shillings' house! The new owner was Michael, a twenty-one-year old EMT. An ambitious, engaging young man, he was eager to own a home. Kate and Lou would much approve of his taking over *The Homestead.*

At the end of the closing, Jamey presented him with the keys to the house. My generous husband then gave the buyer keys to Lou's riding lawnmower.

"Here you go, Michael. It's all yours. If you have any trouble starting the mower, give me a call. It can be ornery."

"Thank you, sir."

As we were leaving, I asked Michael if he'd be interested in seeing a photo of the Shillings.

"Yes, ma'am. I'd like that."

I opened to the pictures on my cellphone and found the one of them posing in front of their home.

"Why, it's Miss Kate!" exclaimed Michael.

"You know her?"

"Yes, ma'am. She lives at Hollander, right?"

"Right."

"Miss Kate has ridden in my ambulance a couple of times. She's a real nice lady."

"Thank you for saying that, Michael. Miss Kate will be very pleased you bought her home."

"Tell her Michael says, 'hey.'"

"I will."

Admittedly, this is a very short chapter, however, such a significant triumph deserves the reader's full attention. What are the odds of a home's previous owner taking a ride in the buyer's ambulance?

I salute the Lord's excellent timing along with His delicious sense of irony.

The Phone Call

Hollander called. I saw the phone ID and clutched my neck. As when Lou died, I instinctively sensed something was wrong.

It was Susan. She said, "We're calling an ambulance to take Miss Kate to Athens Regional."

"No! Please don't," I begged. "I'm on my way."

"I'm coming, too," said Jamey.

We rushed to Kate's side and found her terribly confused, much more so than usual.

"Susan, you do understand why we can't take her back to Athens Regional. She gets very agitated there. Is there any other option, please?"

Susan suggested the smaller hospital in Monroe, only ten minutes away.

We helped Kate into Jamey's sedan. Susan hurried inside to alert the hospital that we were on our way. My considerate husband turned his radio on to a classical channel. A lover of music, Kate calmed down. I rubbed her shoulders.

"I'm not myself," she repeated.

"We'll be there soon," I said hopefully. Soon seemed more like forever.

Rubbing her fingers together, Kate said, "There's sand on my hands."

I prayed she wasn't having a stroke.

"My fingers are numb."

Maybe we should have called an ambulance. Michael might have been on duty.

When we arrived, a sympathetic lady hurried out to meet us with a wheelchair. She said, "You gonna be fine, darlin'."

We followed close behind as Kate was whisked into a room. I signed forms and we settled in with her. I rubbed Kate's feet.

Much of the long afternoon remains a blur of medical people coming and going. I do remember exactly how I felt. I was fearful yet relieved, because Kate, Jamey, and I were surrounded by gentle, caring people, people like the folks at Hollander. I was glad we were there. Thanks to Susan, we'd made the best decision.

Kate complained of being cold. We alerted the nurse. Every time we asked for an additional blanket, another one was provided. Our freezing patient was covered with six blankets before she felt warm.

After a couple of hours, Dr. Patel ordered Kate to be taken for an MRI. When she was brought back to her room, the doctor suggested we have her admitted to the hospital for further testing.

"No, please, Dr. Patel, no more tests."

I told her about Athens Regional, about our painful memories of Lou's death there, and how upset her patient tended to get every time she was hospitalized.

The physician's professional demeanor softened. "I agree. It is time."

"Time?"

"Yes, ma'am. It's time for you and your husband to take her home. We'll set up hospice right away."

We took her to Hollander. With the help of the night time staff, we put her to bed. Worn to a frazzle, Kate was asleep before we turned out her light.

Thank You, Hollander.
Thank you, Compassionate Care.

I called Hollander first thing the next morning and was told Compassionate Care Hospice had set up a hospital bed in Kate's bedroom.

"She's resting comfortably."

Kate was nice and warm with no further complaints of sand on her hands. In a day or two, Hollander called to tell me their patient was becoming somewhat alert. Filled with hope, I left at once.

Had I not been certain I was standing in Kate's apartment, I'd have assumed this was the wrong room. Without her glasses and her Georgia baseball hat, I hardly recognized Kate Shilling. All I saw was an unfamiliar, frail old woman.

Why was Kate not sitting in her chair greeting me with, "What a great surprise! Where's Jamey?"

Only two weeks prior, she and I had been sitting in the lobby chatting about nothing of any significance. We were simply enjoying one another's company. Oree spoke to us, as did Sue, and Marvin, too. She bid me goodbye from her wheelchair.

We kissed. I turned back and kissed her again. I almost took her picture. I didn't, assuming I'd take one another time.

"See you next week," she said.

"Next week."

"I love you."

"I love you, too."

The following week Jamey and I did return. Tragically, it was to rush Kate to the emergency room. There would be no cheerful picture of her waving goodbye.

I looked down at Kate. I couldn't believe how much she'd changed.

"I'm here, Kate. I'm here with you." Even though her eyes were shut, I moved Lou's picture closer.

I think back to the phone call saying Kate was becoming alert. I now realize the caring Hollander people, knowing I was an hour away, didn't want to alarm me. They knew I'd drive more safely to Kate's side, if I expected to see her feeling better. Thank you, sweet, thoughtful friends.

Two ladies from Compassionate Care Hospice came in greeting me cordially and introducing themselves.

"Thank you for making Kate comfortable. I'm completely stunned by her decline. How do you think she's doing?"

"We're glad you're already here, Mrs. Propst. We were going to call to have you come right away."

I don't recall what words either lady used. They both were soft spoken and composed. What remained emblazoned on my mind is the phrase, "The end is near."

"The end?"

"Yes, perhaps within a few days."

"A few days?"

Kate became agitated. Her eyes remained tightly shut and she was speaking with a garbled language none of us understood. I don't know if the Hospice ladies remained or not. I was too focused on Kate. I stood at her side taking her hand in mine. Frozen in place, I lost track of the time.

Sue, her dedicated housekeeper, was leaving town for a week at the beach.

"I just know Miss Kate will pass while I'm gone."

"Kate's a fighter. She may be right here when you get back," I responded.

After the straightforward evaluation from the Hospice ladies, I realized Kate wasn't going to survive for Sue's return. She realized it, too. Neither of us said so out loud. Maybe if gone unsaid, it wouldn't happen.

I offered Sue Lou's prized photograph of the cardinal.

"Cardinals always remind me of my two boys. You know both of them are gone now."

"I remember, Sue. I'm truly sad about your sons."

"Whenever I see a cardinal, I think of my boys." She clutched Lou's picture to her chest.

We hugged tightly.

As Sue left to get back to work, I said, "I want you and your family to have a great time together. You deserve it."

"We will."

Again, I stood beside Kate. "I'm still here."

I almost expected my feisty little nun to reply with a twinkle, "So am I!"

She didn't.

I brushed back her hair and stood sentry. It was as hot as blue blazes outside. Our summer had been a brutal one. I looked through the window at the big expanse of land in front of Hollander Senior Living.

"Kate, do you think this property was once somebody's farm? Were there cattle grazing out there? Can you imagine them wandering down to the pond for a drink of water? Maybe our ducks quacked angrily at a thirsty cow or two for disturbing their peace."

After a little while I checked my watch and leaned closer to Kate. "I'd better get ahead of the afternoon traffic. It's Friday. You know how bad Fridays can be."

Kate's eyelids fluttered.

How I yearned for her to beg me to stay.

Her eyelids fluttered again. I leaned down touching her face.

"I love you, Kate Shilling."

Kate struggled to speak. I made believe she said, "I love you, too."

As time goes by, I'm certain she did.

The Wizard of Oz

Kate Shilling managed to survive the weekend. Encouraged, I hoped she'd prove wrong the dire predictions of her eminent death. I was being overly optimistic. When I walked in Monday, I was greeted tenderly by Oree, Nurse Diane, and Tanika. Feeling forewarned, I walked by myself to Apartment 17.

Oxygen tubes were pushed into Kate's nose. How had I not noticed them on Friday?

Surely the tubes were new. It mattered not. I settled into the rocker by her bedside.

"Kate, it's me."

No reply.

"I'm right here. I love you."

Only the hum of oxygen creased the silence.

I walked around her apartment looking at a lifetime of memories, pictures and paintings, an owl coffee mug, the Tallee dog, books, a card from Trudy, her treasured clock, the music box, Linda's Christmas tree, and Kate's Georgia cap. Her hat was sitting on the bookcase, not on her head where it belonged. Our family Christmas card remained on the refrigerator. I sat in her blue recliner but felt as though I were trespassing. It was Kate's chair.

I stood up and looked at Lou's picture. "Are you on your way?"

I decided to go home. I was doing nothing to help my nun. Seeing her only brought back how dreadful Lou appeared eleven months prior, and he was dead. DEAD. As I went into Kate's bedroom to bid my leave, visitors began to arrive. I was glad I'd stayed.

The first to poke his head around Kate's bedroom door was Marvin. He was visibly upset.

"I always liked Miss Kate," he said. "I like all the folks here, but Miss Kate, well, she's somebody special."

Next to come were the Hospice ladies, including Kimberly, Kate's nurse.

Afterwards, Micah, her Physical Therapist, arrived. He is a tremendous Georgia fan and appreciated Kate's enthusiasm for UGA football.

He asked, "Did you know Miss Kate taught the great Herschel Walker?"

"No! Really?"

"That's what she told me," said the PT, "It had to be true because she said it so many times!"

Here was yet another interesting tidbit about Kate.

Micah added, "Miss Kate said Herschel was a sweet young man."

"Surely sounds like something she'd point out, 'sweet young man'!"

I couldn't wait to add that to my list of Kate stories. It became a favorite, along with Nedom's revelation about our nun's being his baseball pitcher and, of course, Sister's warning to Flannery O'Connor to NOT write about her!

As visitors arrived, I was reminded of the final scene in *The Wizard of Oz* when characters from Auntie Em's Kansas farming community showed up outside Dorothy's bedroom window. When the injured girl saw the three farmhands (the Scarecrow, the Tin Man, and the Cowardly Lion along with the Wizard, himself), she exclaimed, "You and you and you and you were there!" (in the Land of Oz)

Unlike like Dorothy, however, Kate did not speak. I only hoped she was somehow aware of the presence of those dear people who cared about her. Kate had made more new friends during the previous eleven months of her life than she had for the past forty plus years.

As the morning turned into afternoon, Kate's eyes remained closed. She wasn't responding. There was no sound other than her deepening cough.

"She's really not with us anymore," whispered Patience, the appropriately named Hospice nurse.

I asked if Kate might have pneumonia. When my own mother was dying, the physician termed pneumonia as the terminally ill patient's "friend."

Patience, assuring me Kate did not have pneumonia, became quite upset.

"Oh dear, I hope she's not allergic. After her bath this morning, I powdered her up pretty good."

"Patience, I can promise you, she has no allergy to baby powder!" It felt good to loosen up a little bit. "Kate delights in using ample amounts of that stuff!"

Shashandra was the last staff member to drop by. The energetic young lady was forever trying to amuse Miss Kate. Once she convinced my nun to let her paint her nails with bright pearl pink polish.

Kate finally relented and Shashandra went to work.

When she was finished, I exclaimed, "Kate, your nails look beautiful!"

"How do you like them, Miss Kate?" asked the manicurist.

"I feel like a floozy," she complained.

"But your nails are lovely," I insisted.

"I don't like them."

Shrugging her shoulders, Shashandra immediately reached for a cotton ball and the polish remover.

"That's better," acknowledged Kate.

I reminded the darling young lady of the manicure. We both chuckled but only for a brief moment. Shashandra leaned over and kissed Kate. "I love you."

After she left, I rested my cheek on Kate's. Warm to the touch, she still smelled of baby powder.

The phone call came around midnight. I flew to our kitchen.

"I am sorry to tell you. Mrs. Shilling has passed away."

Numb. I was crushed. My teacher was gone. She died on August 15, the Feast of Our Lady of the Assumption. To heck with money worries, I wanted her back with me. I dropped to the floor and wept.

The Visitor

The next few days were a flurry of messages and phone calls following my Facebook posting about Kate's death. I understood she'd disapprove and why, but I needed support from my friends, especially from those who'd known Sister Thomas Margaret.

I traveled to Highlands for a long scheduled two-day trip with Pam and Jackie to visit our friend, Betty. How like Kate to time her death so I could be with the girls. My demeanor was definitely more somber than usual. I wasn't totally engaged with my friends but they understood. A dreary day of rain echoed my deepening sorrow. Mercifully, on the following morning, a long walk in the cool mountain air refreshed my shattered spirits.

Had I not begged the Angel of Death to come for Kate? Shame on me. SHAME!

When we were on our way home, Nurse Susan called.

"I can't believe Miss Kate died!"

"Neither can I, Susan. I'm so sad. I know you are."

"I am."

Susan told me she'd visited Kate on Saturday and was shocked by how much she'd gone downhill in a few short days.

"Everything happened too fast," I lamented. "Kate was perfectly fine a couple of weeks ago."

"I know. When I saw her lying there in the hospital bed," Susan began, "I almost lost my breath."

"Me, too."

There was a pause as we both tried to gather our emotions.

"I want to tell you about my visit with her on Saturday," said Susan.

"Please do."

"I was standing by her bed, when all of a sudden, Miss Kate's arms reached up high in the air."

"Reached?"

"Yes, ma'am, you better believe it! She was holding up those arms, just talking her little heart out."

"To whom?"

"I don't know. I couldn't understand a thing she was saying. But Miss Kate surely saw something above her bed."

"Kate must have been talking to Lou!"

"My goodness!"

I envisioned Lou, young and healthy, beckoning to his wife. "Come on, Scout. I'm taking you to Heaven with me."

I will be forever grateful to Susan for sharing the beautiful, hope-filled image with me. Kate didn't die by herself. Yes, she had nurses and caregivers. Best of all, however, she had her beloved husband, Lou.

Part of me wonders if she left with Lou on Saturday after Susan's visit.

Clearing Out Kate's Apartment

I anticipated a depressing and labor intense day when Jamey and I went to empty out Kate's apartment. At my friend Pam's suggestion, I'd encouraged the Hollander people to select items they might like to have as a remembrance of their beloved Miss Kate.

"Susan wants to give Kate's television to another resident."

"Good plan. She's hardly watched it the last few months. It's practically brand new."

"She never understood how to work the clicker," I laughed. "Changing channels had always been Lou's job."

Jamey was quiet as he stewed about our day ahead. Typically for me, I continued to nervously run my mouth.

"Susan missed out on getting her painting of the horses. She wasn't working the day the others selected their items," I said. "I'm sorry the person, who was devoted to Kate and to me, was disappointed. I hope she'll agree to accept the rocking chair."

"Maybe so."

I often sat in that chair, rocking back and forth, telling Kate what day it was and assuring her Tallee was happy. She'd look at her watch to check if it were getting close to meal time. It was in the rocker I spent my last moments with Kate. I wanted someone special to have it. Susan was the ideal recipient.

I wished I could answer all of Kate's questions----one last time.

"It's Wednesday."

"Tallee is doing fine with Cassie."

"Yes, Kate, I'll be back next week."

"Most of the furniture can go to Goodwill," said Jamey as we drove down Hog Mountain Road. "We may have to take some of her stuff to the Athens city dump."

"Whatever you decide," I offered automatically.

I glanced out the window at the farms peppering either side of the road. I'd miss that quiet part of the drive, the peaceful stretch of rolling green farmland with its goats and the three donkeys, who seemed to acknowledge me whenever I passed.

We turned onto Highway 78. On our right was the big house up on the hill. I spotted the wonderful old farm to our left.

I loved that homestead and keep of photograph of it in an album. For Christmas, the family hangs wreaths in the farmhouse windows. I would miss those familiar sights. Mostly I would miss Kate Shilling.

When we walked through the front door of Hollander, Tanika said she had something for me. She placed Kate's wedding ring into my hand.

"Thank you, Tanika."

"Every day Miss Kate came to the desk to sign in even though she didn't need to. I'd give her a pen. She often signed in more than once!"

"Always a rule follower," I said, "but only if she believed the rules were justified."

I took off my own rings and slid Kate's onto my finger. The action felt like a rite of passage, almost sacramental. I replaced my rings merging them together. I could sense the warmth of Kate's soft hands. Was she beside me still signing the guest book?

I'd already gathered some of the Shillings' personal belongings including the books they'd spent a decade writing, pictures, and Lou's painting of *The Madonna*.

Jamey and I walked toward Apartment 17. How strange it was to enter the emptiness of a "Kate-less" apartment. In September, Jamey and I worried our association with Hollander Senior Living might last beyond her money. Tears filled my eyes as I realized the time had passed all too quickly.

Jamey jumped in with both feet and started putting discards in bags. I stood by helplessly, unable to make any decisions.

"So much is still here," I groaned.

"I told you we'd have to go to the dump."

At that very moment, the Lord sent us a message. Marie came down the hall singing *Amazing Grace*.

"How great Thou art . . ."

The Activities Director was belting out one of my favorite hymns. At first, she appeared a bit embarrassed.

"Marie, your hymn is such a gift. Please continue. We need your angelic voice this morning."

To my delight she again sang *Amazing Grace*. That time she sang it for us. Maybe the day wasn't going to be difficult after all.

Sue and Marvin offered their assistance. Of course, they did. Sue and Marvin were always helping Kate and me. For example, the kindhearted maintenance man wound up Miss Kate's mantel clock every single afternoon for eleven months without fail.

My cellphone buzzed. Lanie, Kate's OT, was texting me.

Good morning!! Yes, I was able to pick up my painting. I am so blessed to have this gift from such an amazing lady. Thank you for it!! Her room has been picked over a good bit. I did get a picture on her wall that complemented the colors of the painting and a small rock she had on her dresser. If you want either of these items, or if they were promised to anyone else, I will get them back to Hollander immediately. I saw her book, *To Kill a Mockingbird*, which I remember was her favorite. Her husband called her "Scout." That made me cry. We really had some sweet conversations. She was so kind and easy to love. Thank you for the pictures. I love them!!!

If you have any photos or pictures, furniture, or extra items from her room, once you pack up everything, please think of me. Bree and I are starting out without a thing because of my divorce. Just keep it in the back of your mind. Anything is needed, furniture, bed frames, anything. Please file it back, in case you have to get rid of things. Thank you again for my painting. I love it. I will hang it in my room over my bed when I get one.

Have a blessed day!!! Lanie

Earlier in the Spring Lanie asked if she could bring her daughter Bree to meet Miss Kate, whom she referred to as "her very special patient." Of course, I said she could. By then, Kate enjoyed company, especially the company of young people.

"Miss Kate rose to the occasion," said Lanie. "She worked very hard with Bree on her painting skills. The two of them discussed art and the use of color. Miss Kate spent a great deal of time with my daughter. I'm so thankful. It's a memory Bree and I will cherish always."

As it turned out, it was Lanie's daughter, Bree, not this writer, who became Kate's very last student. I rejoice!

*By the week's end, Lanie arranged to have all of Kate's remaining furniture picked up for her. There would be no truck rental and no trip to the dump.

"One thing is for sure," announced Jamey, as he tied up a garbage bag of unusable clothing. "I will be taking that ceramic dog back to Goodwill where it belongs."

"Or I may bring her home with us so she can haunt you, Jamey Propst!"

We were finishing up in the living room, when Lanie texted again.

I have one last favor to ask. Does anyone else want the cute little dog sitting by Miss Kate's television?

I immediately texted her back. She's all yours, Lanie. You can retrieve Kate's pooch when you come for your furniture.

Like the living, breathing Tallee, the lucky ceramic pup would be rescued once again!

Another Question Answered

I have a childhood friend, Linda Lehner Holman, with whom I reconnected when our teenagers were students at Marist School in Atlanta. During the 1950's, Linda was my swimming instructor at Camp Marymount in Fairview, Tennessee. She recently purchased a couple of my books and invited me to have brunch with some of her friends, including her sister, Catherine. Ours was a long, delicious, and very chatty meal.

Linda asked how my nun was doing. I relayed the sad news about Kate's death.

"I'm so sorry!"

"Me, too. But it's comforting to know Kate is in Heaven with her husband."

"Husband?" questioned one of the ladies. "I thought you said this person was a nun?"

"That's right," I explained. "When Kate met Lou Shilling, she was a Sister of St. Joseph. Even so, they fell head over heels in love. I'm actually working on a book about them."

"I can't wait to read that one!" said the ever encouraging Linda.

Catherine asked, "Was Lou a Catholic priest?"

"Yes, he was. How could you know?"

"I was a friend of his sister."

"Trudy? You know Trudy!"

"Yes, she's a doll. Trudy and I went to Visitation together. I was at Father Shilling's ordination."

"You were? I've been trying to pinpoint the year Lou was ordained."

"Easy," replied Catherine, "It was 1959."

I was so excited about Catherine's connection with Trudy, I emailed her as soon as I got home. Trudy responded quickly asking for her former classmate's address. I can imagine the two of them enjoyed quite a long conversation!

I wonder if Catherine admitted to Trudy that she often referred to her handsome brother as "Father What-a-Waste"?

A Shrine

The cremation people called. "Mrs. Shilling is ready."

I wished she was really ready, ready for lunch or ready for a drive through the Maple Forge subdivision. Mrs. Shilling was not ready. She was being held captive in a small container. The very idea makes me cringe.

We'd had Lou's cremains delivered by the U.S. Post Office, which felt even worse. Neither of us was thinking very clearly at the time. I'd placed his cremains in our entry hall atop Tallee's crate, along with his crucifix, and Trudy's orchid. The shrine stayed in place until we delivered Tallee to Cassie. Lou had remained in our guest room ever since. I found his presence oddly comforting.

There's a quiet chapel in the funeral home. Cradling Kate's cremains, I stepped inside to offer a prayer. Still reeling from the past couple of weeks, I cannot recall a word I prayed. Maybe I just held the box close to my chest.

At home I reverently placed Kate's cremains on my great grandmother's marble top buffet. I lit a candle and put Kate's Easter orchid near the growing shrine. Lastly, I added three pictures of Kate, one was of her when she taught at St. Pius. The "un-nunny nun" sits on Santa's lap in our school cafeteria. The second was of our high school newspaper staff. The third was a photo of Kate and me, one Linda took in December. She is wearing her University Georgia cap and smiling.

After a couple of days, I took Kate's cremains to the guest room to be near Lou. Neither of them was really there. Were they?

Red Box

Out of the clear blue, I remembered a large cardboard box, one which we'd stored in our basement. As if I were being drawn downstairs, I went right to the box and opened it.

Among the ordinary books and kitchen items was a red container filled with photographs. Months ago, I'd quickly rifled through it only to find dozens and dozens of pictures of mountain landscapes, close-ups of flowers, and numerous shots from Athens Botanical Gardens. I thought about the Shillings' defunct greeting card business and chuckled. A very smart man, Lou never had been much of an entrepreneur.

I carried the red box upstairs to further inspect the contents. Emptying it onto our dining room table, I set to one side the photos of scenery, flowers, and of the Shilling dogs. Included were Tallee, several labs, both black and yellow in color, a couple of mutts, and the mixed breed Dalmatian, who Kate insisted sang along with Renee Fleming.

"My word!"

"Have you struck oil?" called out Jamey from his chair in the den.

"Better," I shouted. "There are people in this box!"

Unimpressed, my husband continued watching his football game.

The people stack offered the first gem, a photo of Father Lou Shilling, newly ordained. Thanks to my St. Pius yearbooks, I already had several of Sister Thomas Margaret wearing her habit, or, as she termed it, the outfit.

I found pictures from both from their childhoods. Such adorable little children were they!

There is one photo marked "our honeymoon." Kate and Lou, contentedly smiling, are posed at Stone Mountain Park near Atlanta. Another captures the couple celebrating Lou's receiving his Ph.D. in Psychology. A proud Kate gazes adoringly at her husband.

The stack also included several tourist-themed snapshots of the Shillings' travels throughout New England. Likely the two were excitedly compiling research for their books on Emily and Col. Higginson.

I felt like a spy as I riffled through their lifetime of pictures. I then came upon a studio photograph of Tom, Kate's late brother. The image made my heart hurt. We'd known about his murder, but looking into Tom's eyes, I sensed anew Kate's intense pain from losing her brother in such a senseless and horrific manner.

Also painful was the discovery of Andy's baby pictures.

There he is, as cute as could be, with his parents and with his grandmother, Isabell. My mind played tricks on me as the Shillings' long lost son stared out from the photo as if to say, "It's okay now. We are at peace."

"I hope that's true, Andy."

Should these pictures be shared? How I wish I could ask the Shillings for their permission. Had Lou's spirit urged me to look in his study's closet that one last time? I remember telling Jamey I wanted to walk through the empty house for a final check. It was then I spotted the container, which was hidden well out of sight on the closet shelf. Was I supposed to find it? Or was this box meant for the Shillings' eyes only?

I brewed a pot of green tea and reached for my favorite mug. Kate had given it to me on one of our first visits to Brevard. I've used the mug so often, the black ink drawing of a little girl has faded to a dull gray. My teabag steeping, I read the words, "Special Friend, the bonds we have are everlasting."

Given Kate's absolute belief in the afterlife, I could imagine her watching over me as I worked on this book. I turned her wedding ring.

"Am I revealing too much about you and Lou?"

In the silence of the moment, I sipped tea. Warm liquid bathed my throat.

I eventually made a decision. I'd share only two photos with the reader, the un-nunny nun and the young priest. The rest of the Shillings' photographs will remain safely in the red box.

Rings of Gold

After Lou died, Kate wanted me to hold on to two items for her. One was Lou's watch, the second was his wedding ring. Following Kate's death, I sent Trudy the watch.

I frequently find myself fingering Kate's wedding ring much the same way she often did. Still connected with her in many ways, I'm comforted by wearing her ring and consoled by the belief she is reunited with her husband.

I recently retrieved Lou's ring from our safe. As if performing a ritual, I put the two rings together, side by side. I closed my eyes for a minute, then placed Kate's ring inside Lou's. Hers nestles sweetly, naturally within his.

"Kate and Lou, as you prayed, you have come full circle."

It was then I noticed an inscription inside Lou's large gold band. It reads, "Scout 7-27-68."

I examined Kate's ring. Her finger was so small the inscription is barely visible. I picked up a magnifying glass. Even then I couldn't quite make out the letters. Shining a flashlight on the inside of her ring and holding the magnifier at an angle, I read, "Lou 7-27-68."

We've known their anniversary was July 27, but the year remained a mystery. Now we know. The gifted Sister of St. Joseph and the brilliant Marist Priest were happily married for nearly half a century.

An amazing grace, indeed, it is.

Scout

Hospice conducted a memorial service at Hollander. It was something Kate and Lou had vetoed, but, selfishly, I needed to hear the minister's gentle words. As well, I was uplifted by the kindness of Kate's caregivers. I like to think the Shillings might have approved the change in plans. I know "Miss Kate" would have appreciated Sue's sitting with me. I certainly did.

A year ago, Kate had exclaimed, "How beautiful!" when I suggested Jamey and I might scatter their ashes together in the mountains. *Together* was what mattered most to her.

Prior to his final act of kindness, Jamey went online to the Catholic Bishops' website. He was searching for the prayers for a proper Catholic graveside service. As he had done when arranging the Last Rites for both Kate and Lou, he was determined to do this correctly.

We timed our ceremony around the Aquarian family birthdays; the Shillings' and mine, Trudy's and her grandson, Chris's.

Similar to the pristine days the Shillings took photographs along the Blue Ridge Parkway, our drive took place on a sunny

February morning. There was an invigorating crispness in the air. Everything felt right to me. On we drove, chatting happily about visits with the Shillings before the onset of Kate's dementia.

After a while, Jamey pulled off at an overlook. He carried a canvas tote bag containing the cremains up a quiet trail as I followed silently behind him. We stopped at the edge of a particularly lovely setting. Together Jamey and I read the prayers. I added a few personal comments of my own. We opened one container, then the next. A gentle breeze carried away the intertwined souls of Kate and Lou.

The moment was simple and private, everything they'd requested.

Kate and Lou will be together now, forever and a day.

Jamey had me pose by a stone bench to commemorate the event. He handed me the canvas bag.

"Milam, look at the brand name."

How could I not have noticed the label when placing the two boxes in the bag? It features a dog logo. Even better, the bag was made by a company called "Scout."

"Are you hungry?"

"Starving."

Jamey and I walked into the lodge atop the mountain and settled in seats by a large window. It offered the same grand view as did Kate and Lou's final resting place. Closing my eyes, I imagined the Shillings seated with us and thought to myself how much they would enjoy the restaurant. Lou would have taken numerous photographs. Upon arriving back home, he would have edited his pictures, while Kate penned a lovely poem to commemorate our day.

Instead, the Shillings are in Heaven, free, young again, and healthy. In my opinion, this makes for a perfect ending.

The following is a gift to the reader from Kate.

Dawn and Dusk in the Blue Ridge Mountains

The Dawn is silver in the morning sky.
She comes on tiptoe through the forest green,
Spilling sparkles from her basket making shadows die.
And then with one great burst of fire
She scales the mountain ridge to pierce the clouds
With silver rays while calling to the world,
"Cast off your nighttime shrouds."

The Dusk is golden in the evening sky.
He comes sure-footed as the Forest glows,
Casting golden coins as he goes.
And then with one great burst of fire
He lights the clouds, then snuffs them out
To give the world to night's desire
For rest upon God's heart.

Together We Will Go

I wonder which of us is stronger
When it becomes the time
To make eternal climb
Which leaves behind our finite space
And goes beyond our human race.
Will you step first
In universal harmony
Or will first going there
Be given me?
Or will this passage feel
The step of two
Who having lived as one on earth
With one ideal of love pass through
This earthy maze of counted days
To fusion of a spirit-birth?
No matter what the circumstance,
Our going will be whole
To our twin soul.

Catherine Small Shilling